REPUTATION CAPITAL

REPUTATION CAPITAL

How to Navigate Crises and Protect Your Greatest Asset

T.J. Winick

BK®

Berrett–Koehler Publishers, Inc.

Berrett-Koehler Publishers, Inc.
1333 Broadway, Suite 1000
Oakland, CA 94612-1921
Tel: (510) 817-2277
Fax: (510) 817-2278
www.bkconnection.com

Ordering Information
Quantity sales. Special discounts are available on quantity purchases by corporations, associations, and others. For details, contact the "Special Sales Department" at the Berrett-Koehler address above.
Individual sales. Berrett-Koehler publications are available through most bookstores. They can also be ordered directly from Berrett-Koehler: Tel: (800) 929-2929; Fax: (802) 864-7626; www.bkconnection.com.
Orders for college textbook/course adoption use. Please contact Berrett-Koehler: Tel: (800) 929-2929; Fax: (802) 864-7626.

Distributed to the U.S. trade and internationally by Penguin Random House Publisher Services.

Berrett-Koehler and the BK logo are registered trademarks of Berrett-Koehler Publishers, Inc.

Printed in the United States of America

Berrett-Koehler books are printed on long-lasting acid-free paper. When it is available, we choose paper that has been manufactured by environmentally responsible processes. These may include using trees grown in sustainable forests, incorporating recycled paper, minimizing chlorine in bleaching, or recycling the energy produced at the paper mill.

Library of Congress Cataloging-in-Publication Data
Name: Winick, T.J., author.
Title: Reputation capital : how to navigate crises and protect your greatest asset / T.J. Winick.
Description: First edition. | Oakland, CA : Berrett-Koehler Publishers, [2022] | Includes bibliographical references and index.
Identifiers: LCCN 2022010222 (print) | LCCN 2022010223 (ebook) | ISBN 9781523001842 (paperback ; alk. paper) | ISBN 9781523001859 (pdf) | ISBN 9781523001866 (epub) | ISBN 9781523001873
Subjects: LCSH: Corporate image. | Reputation. | Public relations. | Scandals. | Crisis management.
Classification: LCC HD59.2 .W56 2022 (print) | LCC HD59.2 (ebook) | DDC 659.2—dc23/eng/20220310
LC record available at https://lccn.loc.gov/2022010222
LC ebook record available at https://lccn.loc.gov/2022010223

First Edition
28 27 26 25 24 23 22   10 9 8 7 6 5 4 3 2 1

Book producer: Linda Jupiter Productions   Editor: Karen Seriguchi
Text designer: Kim Scott, Bumpy Design   Proofreaders: Mary Kanable & Daniel Gall
Cover designer: Matt Avery   Indexer: Liester Indexing
Author photo: Jim Dandee

For K and P, my anchors

CONTENTS

*It takes 20 years to build a reputation
and five minutes to ruin it.*

If you think about that, you'll do things differently.

—WARREN BUFFETT

PREFACE

REPUTATION CAPITAL isn't based on classroom learnings, it isn't a text-book written in the abstract. This is a practical guide informed by my nearly three decades in communications, twenty years of which were spent as a broadcast news reporter and my subsequent—and current—career as a counselor of crisis communications and issues management. When it comes to the media's dogged pursuit of a story, you might say I've been both the *hunter* and the *hunted*.

Among the most memorable stories I covered as a reporter were those focused on an organization or individual in crisis, confronting a potentially reputation-defining dilemma, scandal, or emergency. Some of these events or issues were self-induced through poor decision-making. Others were honest mistakes, accidents, or the result of external forces genuinely beyond the C-suite's control. Regardless, the stakes couldn't have been higher: the reputation and the viability of brands hung in the balance. How those in charge responded in the maelstrom of a raging crisis had the power to bolster, damage, or destroy all that they and their colleagues had worked tirelessly to build.

Crises can include everything from executive misconduct to work-place violence to a product recall: anything that might disrupt operations, place an organization's personnel in danger, or result in a loss of trust. Some of the biggest crises I covered were the British Petroleum (BP) oil spill along the Gulf of Mexico, the Pennsylvania State football scandal, sexual abuse cases involving the Catholic Archdiocese of Boston, and the Toyota recall of 2009–10. Each of these crises claimed multiple victims, destroyed lives, and had a lingering impact on the families, businesses, industries, and leaders (in many cases, now former leaders) at their center.

My career in journalism provided me with a front-row seat to these real-life dramas, reporting on those whose reputation was under assault by internal and external critics. I learned what contributed to effective and ineffective crisis communications and how a brand's reputation—good or bad—was impacted as a result.

I witnessed responses by management teams that fell everywhere along the spectrum from masterful and adept to incompetent and pathetic. Some leaders mismanaged crises and communicated in a manner so tone-deaf that it was genuinely difficult to comprehend how they'd risen to a position of prominence in such demanding and competitive industries. Other leaders navigated a crisis with such cool confidence, it was as if they had a playbook for that very scenario.

Inevitably, some leaders are done in by their own pride; they're combative with the media and anyone else who happens to question their decision-making. Assuming a defensive posture and tone, these executives appear more focused on picking a fight or settling a score with anyone who even remotely suggests assigning responsibility than to solving the crisis at hand.

So, is there a secret sauce to maintain a pristine reputation in the face of adversity? The answer is never that simple. Any successful strategy to protect a reputation must begin with the time, effort, and energy a brand has put into cultivating the trust, admiration, and loyalty of its key constituents.

Then, when disaster does hit, that groundwork—coupled with ample crisis planning undertaken ahead of time—will ensure a brand remains unscathed. One thing, however, is clear: Withstanding significant reputational damage rarely depends on an organization's size or available resources. More important are the ability to relate to and empathize with others and to maintain a strong moral compass, a true north to guide leaders when times get tough.

How an organization responds to and communicates at a challenging time will always represent a fork in the road. Choosing the correct path can make all the difference. One direction can help a company build back its reputation; the other can result in it being torn down completely.

I hope this book will help you, the reader, gain a greater understanding of what goes into protecting your greatest asset—your reputation—and, when faced with a threat, how you can avoid the mistakes, missteps, and false moves that can lead to its demise. My experiences, studying both those who got it wrong *and* those who got it right, inform the recommendations on these pages. It's far better to learn these lessons before your reputation comes under fire than to suddenly try to reinvent your business or your brand in the midst of chaos.

Far too many leaders dig themselves deeper into trouble with lies or denial rather than put their integrity first. However, by making the right moves, you can protect your reputation—perhaps even enhance it—after emerging from the crucible of a true crisis.

INTRODUCTION

CONFESSIONS OF A FORMER REPORTER

It's 4 p.m. on a Thursday in September when a series of explosions rocks three neighboring New England towns. Dozens of house fires break out, thousands of residents are forced to evacuate, twenty-two are injured, and one young man is killed. As news helicopters hover overhead, emergency responders scramble on the ground and thick plumes of smoke cloud the sky. The source: excessive pressure in a subterranean natural gas line, later confirmed by a federal investigation.[1]

State and local officials try repeatedly, and unsuccessfully, to reach the utility company, Columbia Gas of Massachusetts. Reporters dial a hotline that plays a recorded voice message; the utility company is closed.[2] Four long hours after the initial explosion, the company issues its first public statement, but doesn't say what went wrong. The next day, Columbia Gas representatives hold a brief press conference. They offer conflicting information, appearing woefully unprepared for even the most obvious questions. Their statements don't soothe. Instead, they fuel concern and further worry.

THIS TERRIFYING SCENARIO, describing the Merrimack Valley gas explosions of 2018, left the reputation of Columbia Gas of Massachusetts in ruins. Its initial response was so disappointing, the governor put its competitor, Eversource, in charge of restoration efforts. In the end, Columbia pleaded guilty to violating safety standards and agreed to pay a $53 million criminal fine plus $143 million to settle multiple class-action lawsuits.[3] As part of the federal plea deal, parent company NiSource was forced to sell Columbia to Eversource.

The catastrophe itself, while preventable, wasn't the sole reason Columbia's reputation was left in tatters. It was largely due to a response that was incompetent and appeared indifferent; one that didn't seem urgent when lives were on the line, wasn't *transparent* when public safety was at risk, wasn't *accountable* when answers were needed, and wasn't *empathetic* as many residents were displaced. The company's crisis response was severely lacking in the critical first hours—inexcusable and downright unfathomable in a heavily regulated and public-facing industry whose product is a highly volatile substance.

● ● ●

During my career in broadcast news, I couldn't have imagined myself in any other line of work. I was addicted to the adrenaline of breaking news, of always working against the deadline of the next newscast. Regardless of what station I worked at, I appreciated the special bond and camaraderie this joint mission forged among my colleagues and me. We considered ourselves on a noble quest—to pursue the truth and to educate our viewers—all while feeling grateful we weren't working 9-to-5 desk jobs.

I loved the creative process of producing a news story: writing a script to convey the most important information and matching those words to the video footage the camera person and I captured in the field. I relished the access afforded me as a journalist and appreciated the challenge of translating complex issues into language our viewers could easily process and understand.

What wasn't apparent to me at the time was that my journalism career would be the ideal training ground for my second career in strategic and crisis communications, where I would help organizations navigate the very type of crises I'd been reporting on, day in, day out.

Chief among the skills I honed: an understanding of how public perception of a brand can be bolstered or sullied at these moments and an appreciation for how an effective and decisive leader makes decisions at times of great stress.

For instance, if it's a fatal industrial accident, I can now anticipate how the press will first report on the basics of the accident; what's referred to as the *who, what, where, when, why,* and *how* of a news event. I know that follow-up stories will focus on the victims as reporters reach out to the loved ones they left behind. And then the company itself: Has it been cited for safety infractions before? Will there be fines or penalties imposed by inspectors and regulators? Will there be criminal charges for negligence?

Before I said goodbye to broadcast journalism, I spoke with dozens of former colleagues: reporters, producers, and editors who had successfully made their own career transition. Each was encouraging, assuring me the skills acquired and polished over years of reporting were relevant in the private and public sectors. They'd be helpful in the for-profit and nonprofit worlds, with in-house marketing and communications roles, and at a public relations firm.

They shared that among the most highly coveted and transferable skills was that same ability to interpret complex issues for a mass audience: to act as what one journalist turned public relations practitioner called an "English-to-English translator." They made the case that the deadline-driven writing and presentation skills I took for granted as a journalist would be highly relevant and applicable in the world of public relations, reputation management, and crisis communications.

●   ●   ●

I realized just how relevant these skills were while working with my first two clients.

Our firm was retained by a company that owned a chain of convenience stores. It brought us aboard when it had to fire an employee but feared potential blowback. Why? The employee in question, a cashier at one of the stores, pulled a gun on a knife-wielding robber in self-defense. While he was successful in scaring off the assailant, he had violated company policy, which prohibited any employee from bringing firearms to work. It was the type of vigilante story too juicy for the media to resist: an employee with an otherwise spotless record fired from his job for using a legally owned weapon to defend himself.

Once the local press caught wind of the story, the unassuming former employee was predictably elevated to hero status by many within the community, including Second Amendment activists. I'd been out of journalism for less than a year and could still imagine myself covering the story: tracking down and speaking with the former employee, soliciting what was then referred to as "man on the street" interviews to sample public opinion, and doing whatever was necessary to connect with the employer for an on-camera interview or written statement. Only now I was on the other side of the story, defending the company's decision.

First, my colleague and I asked the client if they would consider reversing their decision and rehiring the individual. They would not. While they weren't out to make an example of the young man, who was a solid employee, they also felt they couldn't make any exceptions. It was clear their position wasn't going to change. I put on my reporting hat and envisioned how this story would play out: protesters would allege that the company didn't care about its employees if it wouldn't let this individual protect himself against an armed robber.

That's why the public statement I drafted directly countered that argument and communicated just the opposite sentiment: it was *because* the company cared so much about the health and well-being of their employees that bringing a firearm to work could simply not be tolerated. Yes, there was a protest in front of the store one afternoon, but the media coverage was contained to one news cycle, and the reputational threat was effectively contained. It was quite a surreal experience when I watched a newscast in which the reporter, a former colleague of mine, read the statement that I'd drafted on behalf of the company.

The second issue involved a global corporation that was to be the subject of a *60 Minutes*–style television exposé. We were escorted into the office of the general manager, who would act as the company's spokesperson for the interview. Though an experienced and admired corporate executive, she was rightfully concerned about how she, and thus the company, would be portrayed. After reviewing some carefully crafted talking points with her, it was clear she'd be a strong advocate. Next, we moved into a mock interview session with me acting as reporter and capturing the exchange on video to be reviewed afterward.

As I sat down in my chair to begin the training, I pulled it right up to the client who was sitting across from me, our knees practically touching. She looked at me with a bewildered expression. I explained that this was a reporter technique: intimidate the interview subject by crowding their space. We ran through a few rounds of questions, and each time, she visibly grew more comfortable and confident in answering a litany of tough questions in tight quarters.

A week later, the GM called to thank me, crediting our practice session for her confidence during the actual interview; she had felt totally prepared during the exchange. The reporter did just as I had predicted, pulling his chair uncomfortably close to hers. When the final story aired, the GM came across as knowledgeable and thoughtful, with reasonable answers and explanations for the issues that the story addressed.

She had successfully put a human face on a company that was being portrayed by the reporter as cold, uncaring, and interested only in the bottom line. As a result of her professional demeanor and effective messages, the story was more balanced than it would have been had she and the company not participated at all. Viewers were left to make up their own minds as to which side had made a stronger case.

● ● ●

Any individual or organization can face a crisis. This book is primarily about reputational threats confronting the latter: corporations, small businesses, nonprofits, state agencies, colleges and universities, and NGOs (nongovernmental organizations such as charities, research institutions, and community and faith-based organizations).

While *organization* refers to an entity with employees and operations that produces a product or sells a service, a *brand* is the personality and public-facing element of that organization. For example, Procter & Gamble is one company with multiple brands, including Tide detergent, Bounty paper towels, and Old Spice deodorant.

In many cases, because the name of the organization and the brand are synonymous (e.g., Apple, Ocean Spray, and Nike), I'll be using terms such as *organization*, *business*, *company*, and *brand* interchangeably in this book. My point is that all have one thing in common: individuals responsible for their success who must sometimes make hard decisions that can determine if the entity prospers or falters.

Whether your position includes a communications function or not, I've written this book so that anyone, from intern up to CEO, can understand the considerations that should be top of mind and the practical tools that should be available when facing a reputational threat. My hope is that, in taking this advice to heart, you and your colleagues will be ready to respond in the eye of the storm. You'll be better equipped to protect and defend your reputation during those moments when everything's on the line.

1

WHAT IS YOUR REPUTATION CAPITAL?

THE NEXT TIME YOU LISTEN TO, read, or watch the news about a brand in crisis, notice how its image inevitably finds its way into the narrative. It's not surprising, since we typically process news about a scandal through a filter that's based on our previous perceptions of the organization, product, or individual. Past actions build expectations for how the brand will carry itself in the future.

If a brand has had issues or been at the center of a previous scandal, phrases like "no stranger to controversy" or "this isn't the first time *Brand X* has caused an uproar among its customers" might very well be part of the story. Conversely, when a trusted brand is in trouble, phrases like "loyal customers," "coveted products," or "industry leader" are often woven into the script.

For instance: In March 2022, The Walt Disney Company, one of the most respected and image-conscious companies in the world, faced a crisis of its own making. Groups of its employees were outraged when CEO Bob Chapek didn't publicly condemn a piece of Florida state legislation called the Parental Rights in Education bill, or what its opponents labeled the "Don't Say Gay" bill.

In his first, heavily criticized statement, Chapek wrote that Disney felt its real influence was "through the inspiring content we produce."[1] However, he would end up apologizing to his LGBTQ employees, writing, "You needed me to be a stronger ally in the fight for equal rights and I let you down. I am sorry."[2] In addition to denouncing the bill, Disney decided to freeze all political donations in the state.

But it didn't end there. In response, Florida's governor, a member of the traditionally business-friendly Republican Party, revoked special tax and self-governing privileges enjoyed by Disney in the state for decades. Regardless of how you feel about the Florida legislation, which is now law, it was a political lightning rod from the very beginning and one that Chapek and Disney had failed to adequately prepare for.

While other, lesser brands may have suffered a significant reputational hit as a result of such a crisis, the strength of the Disney brand remains strong. This is, in part, due to its *reputation capital* as arguably the most trusted family-friendly brand in the world, built over decades through its theme parks, movies, and merchandise.

How well you weather a crisis, and how you'll be perceived post-crisis begins with how the public views your brand (i.e., positively versus negatively) in neutral times. That's why it's critical to spend the necessary time, resources, and energy, not just on honing your craft or perfecting your business model but also on building up your reputation capital. This means leaders behaving responsibly, always with their organization's mission and impact top of mind, so that they make better decisions in the first place and subsequently communicate these intentions.

Reputation capital may be described in a variety of ways, but chief among the themes that run through nearly every definition are:

- its intangibility

- trust as its central component

- its importance in amassing financial capital

One often assumes reputation is a soft asset such as a skilled workforce or intellectual property, which is "not normally recognized in an organization's balance sheet."[3] Yet there's an increasing number of reasons to believe a dollar figure can be assigned to reputation include the following:

- a report released pre-pandemic in January 2020 that found "global executives attribute 63 percent of their company's market value to their company's overall reputation"[4]

- the growing demand for ESG (environmental, social, and governance) investing—with investor decisions based on a company's good deeds—and its greater impact alongside profitability and financial returns

- an oft-cited Harvard Business School study that found a restaurant that boosts its Yelp score by one full star can see its revenue increase by 5 to 9 percent[5]

SOCIALLY UNACCEPTABLE

Conducting research for this book, I considered those brands that were notable for having earned a positive reputation (e.g., Patagonia, Nike, Disney) and a negative one (e.g., Philip Morris, Spirit Airlines, Facebook). As part of this exercise, I googled "Facebook crisis." Here's a small sample of the results:

The 21 (and Counting) Biggest Facebook Scandals of 2018 (Wired)

Updating the Facebook Timeline of Scandal and Strife (Creative First)

How Facebook's Crisis Response Missed the Mark (PR Daily)

How Facebook's Response to Whistleblower Could Make Their Crisis Worse (Forbes)

Safe to say, no single brand is so consistently putting out reputational fires as is the company now known as Meta. Among its past transgressions: failing to keep user information secure, allowing the spread of misinformation on such issues as the 2016 US presidential election and COVID-19 vaccines, facilitating the livestream of a mass murder, and reportedly causing a third of teen girls to feel bad about themselves (due to time spent on Instagram, which is owned by Meta).

All that, alone, would be enough to question what's going on in the corner office, but it's *how* CEO Mark Zuckerberg and the brand have responded to these scandals in public statements, interviews, and congressional hearings that could not lower expectations any further. Lucy Prebble, who wrote the play *ENRON*, about the energy company's scandal, once noted that the tone of Facebook's indignant responses can typically be summed up by three words: "How dare you?"[6]

Take a look at some of Zuckerberg's past statements and you'll notice they're overly defensive and indicative of a brand in denial.

- In response to the Cambridge Analytica scandal: "The reality of running a company of more than 10,000 people is that you're not going to know everything that's going on."[7]

- In response to allegations that Facebook has fueled extremism and misinformation: "I believe that the division we see today is primarily the result of a political and media environment that drives Americans apart."[8]

The constant and consistent inability to accept responsibility or project humility leaves little doubt that its next crisis is just around the corner.

The trust in a company and the public's assumptions about it can serve as a type of armor against reputational threats. If a brand is thoughtfully engaged day-to-day in building its reputation, it's more likely to emerge from even the toughest of challenges relatively unscathed when it comes to public perception. It's no wonder reputation management strategies are most effective when they're put into place long before a threat appears on the horizon.

BUILDING YOUR REPUTATION CAPITAL

You can bank reputation capital like deposits in a rainy-day fund. Here are seven recommendations how to begin doing so.

Prioritize Culture

A strong culture begins with how an organization approaches recruiting, team building, mentoring, and maintaining the overall morale of its employees. This determines their productivity and, as a result, the profitability of the business. Over the long haul, culture and reputation inevitably become intertwined. For instance, if a company has a less-than-stellar reputation, it will have a more difficult time recruiting quality employees, which in turn impacts how those employees and management interact, which in turn can erode key cultural elements such as shared values and standards.

Even during moments of crisis, when there may be great uncertainty, an organization can't afford to neglect its own culture. That means setting the tone from the get-go through enhanced transparency, collaboration, and communication.

Consider how many organizations demonstrated they could not only survive but thrive working remotely during the COVID-19 pandemic. Much of this ability was due to the strong culture they began with at the onset and an understanding that it can't be ignored when times are tough; in fact, just the opposite. Doubling down on culture keeps employees engaged and motivated, translating into a better work product and more confident communication with customers or clients.

It doesn't matter how successful, accomplished, or revered a CEO is. If they ignore or don't believe in the importance of interpersonal relationships and how their management team runs day-to-day operations, their indifference will inevitably come back to haunt them and the reputation of the brand. Think HR complaints, lawsuits, and leaks to the press.

Reflect on Feedback

How you engage with those inside and outside your organization is the most straightforward and organic way to influence how others feel about you. Ask yourself: Is your brand helpful? Is your brand perceived as honest and trustworthy? Does your brand keep its promises? If your brand makes a mistake, does leadership admit as much and hold itself accountable?

Today's consumers have multiple ways to provide feedback in real time. Think about how you conduct research before making personal or professional purchases. Never underestimate the power of reviews left on sites like Yelp, Glassdoor, and Amazon. When poor customer service results in negative reviews, they can snowball if not addressed promptly and appropriately.

Monitor what's being said about your brand anywhere a supporter might be building you up or a critic might be tearing you down. Try to address a complaint or concern directly. You'll visibly demonstrate that you take criticism seriously and care enough to rectify issues.

Just don't think a boilerplate statement composed of corporate-speak will get the job done. If online posters believe you're merely paying them lip service, it might make matters worse. In some cases, no reply might actually do less damage than one that's perceived as uncaring and thoughtless. I'll address when and when *not* to respond to criticism in greater detail in chapter 9.

WHOLE FOODS: A FRESH APPROACH TO CRITICISM

In 2003, the director of an animal rights group approached Whole Foods CEO John Mackey at the company's annual meeting and demanded that the supermarket stop buying duck meat from factory farms that treated waterfowl inhumanely. The two exchanged emails and started an open discussion.

Months later, Mackey acknowledged that these conversations had persuaded him to become a vegan, and that "Whole Foods pledged to design humane standards for animals whose meat will be sold in its stores."[9]

In 2015, Mackey sat down to discuss this inflection point in his personal and professional life. What he shared was remarkable for a Fortune 500 CEO in his ability to hear and accept criticism and make real change rather than excuses.

"At the time, I believed Whole Foods Market already had the best animal welfare standards of any food retailer in the US," he told a reporter. "I was taken aback by some of her harsh criticism, but I accepted her challenge to become better informed about animal welfare. . . . By the end of the summer, I realized she was absolutely right—I was horrified by what I had learned."[10]

Not every executive listens to critics with an open mind and an open heart. Though Mackey believed his market had the most ethical animal husbandry practices in the industry, he overcame the impulse to fight back. The revelation persuaded Whole Foods to tighten its standards—and its market share continued to grow. Between 2008 and 2017, the number of locations increased from 275 to nearly 500.[11]

Become a Thought Leader

Work to make your CEO and other executives a go-to person in a reporter's or other influencer's list of contacts. When journalists write a story on a particular industry trend or a conference organizer is putting together a panel of industry heavyweights, they need experts who can provide context, analysis, and insight. They can presumably reach out to *anyone* in, or associated with, the industry, such as analysts or researchers who work for a trade group or a government agency. So when a brand representative appears in a news story or speaks at a prominent event, readers and attendees perceive them as a subject matter expert and a standout leader in their field.

Consider that consumers view earned media (appearing in a third-party news source based on merit and not money) as more trustworthy than advertising. In fact, a 2019 report found that only half of consumers trust paid ads, while 92 percent say they trust earned media.[12]

Additionally, a brand should leverage channels like its own blog, Medium, and the LinkedIn Publishing Platform to share thoughts on relevant ideas and issues to articulate its unique approach and value. This complements earned-media coverage without having to rely on the traditional press to disseminate important messages.

Cultivate an Online Audience

Brands can't wait until a threat emerges or a crisis occurs to begin a dialogue with their followers on a channel that's remained relatively dormant. They must spend the time necessary to establish a unique voice across those social media platforms followed most closely by key constituents. Encouraging a back-and-forth with followers helps brands earn online credentials by cultivating a reputation of accessibility.

In the event of a product recall, data breach, or outage, these pages and feeds tend to be the first places those impacted will turn for information and answers. If a business has established itself as trustworthy and responsive, these channels can be integral in assisting those in need and sharing vital information.

Today's most respected brands excel at online customer service, and this extends to social media. To illustrate this point: One afternoon, a few years ago, I was crossing a busy city street when a brand-new pair of glasses fell off my face and onto the ground. As I safely made it to the curb, I turned around just in time to see them crushed by the tire of a passing vehicle.

I sat back down at my desk and posted an image of the cracked lenses and twisted frames on Instagram, tagging Warby Parker, the company from whom I had purchased them just a week earlier. A representative from the eyewear company wrote me back within an hour, and I had a new pair of glasses, free of charge, less than a week later. Not surprisingly, I remain a loyal customer to this day.

Create Content

Every organization today, no matter its focus, is its own media company with the ability to create videos, infographics, podcasts, blogs, e-books, and other collateral that are free to access and that demonstrate the brand's value. By establishing a rapport with the consumer that isn't solely transactional in nature, the greater the likelihood of building a long-lasting (and eventually profitable) relationship.

Many brands use this content to employ the type of storytelling once traditionally reserved for the press to humanize their businesses and make it more relatable. For example, posting employee and passenger-centric videos such as "A Day in the Life of a Flight Attendant" and "How We De-ice a Plane," which aren't focused merely on cheap fares, helps Southwest Airlines distinguish itself from other low-cost carriers. It's a soft sell that entertains and informs while establishing a visceral connection with personal and business travelers alike.

One of the original pieces of creative content dates back to 1895, when John Deere, the agricultural equipment company, published a journal called *The Furrow*.[13] Along with information about Deere products, it mainly focuses on agricultural news and provides solutions to issues that plague professional farmers and lawn-care enthusiasts. The company understood that producing something that its customers would enjoy reading and come to depend on could be just as valuable as a catalog of the latest products and equipment.

Exercise Corporate Social Responsibility

Initiatives aimed at impacting society in a positive way can include everything from a business donating a percentage of its profits to a worthy cause to efforts to reduce its carbon footprint to a hiring process focused on diversifying its workforce. Yet today's savvy consumer can recognize *virtue signaling* (the insincere attempt to demonstrate you're well-intentioned) or *purpose washing* (the disingenuous embracing of a greater cause), so be prepared to deliver on your promises when committing to be an advocate.

Don't settle for writing a check or engaging in activities that are more performative than substantive. Strive instead to volunteer time, author opinion pieces that shine a light on the causes your business cares about, sit on boards of like-minded organizations, and talk about your brand's commitment earnestly online and elsewhere to raise awareness.

While your organization can choose to support any cause or non-profit, consider those closely aligned with your mission. For a bank, per-haps it's establishing financial literacy for young students with visits to local schools. A residential real estate developer can combat homeless-ness by partnering with nonprofits that work with landlords to prevent evictions. Food manufacturers or restaurant groups can help combat food insecurity through organizations such as World Central Kitchen, which mobilized in response to COVID-19 and has delivered meals in regions hit hard by natural disasters.

Choose a Highest Value

One of corporate America's most respected CEOs is also one of its sharp-est critics. Marc Benioff of Salesforce has gone so far as to call for a "new capitalism," in which brands don't just take from society but also give back, insisting the idea that a business must decide between profit or pur-pose is a false choice.[14]

Accumulating reputation capital is a natural by-product of such a philosophy, one in which a brand regularly demonstrates and commu-nicates that it's not just out for itself and that it views its employees, cus-tomers, and corporate partners as part of one large ecosystem. Central to this, Benioff suggests, is that every CEO chooses an ideal such as *safety*, *truth*, *trust*, or *responsibility* as their highest value and then figures out how to effectively operationalize it.[15]

Although choosing a highest value can cost a brand revenue and mar-ket share in the short term, the understanding is that it will pay off in the long term: the fostering of a better workplace culture leads to the recruit-ment of better employees, which leads to better service, thus making the brand more attractive to potential customers.

A business that's continually on a concurrent journey toward profitability *and* improving the planet will be less likely to generate crises of its own making. It will also be more insulated against reputational damage when one does occur.

For example, CVS Caremark's highest value is health. That's why, in 2014, the company received universal praise for announcing that its more than 7,600 drugstores nationwide would stop selling cigarettes, cigars, and chewing tobacco.[16] It might seem like a no-brainer for a healthcare provider (i.e., not feeding a nicotine habit that will lead to negative health outcomes), but when you're talking about a projected loss of $1.5 billion in annual revenue, the decision couldn't have been arrived at easily.[17] According to CVS's president at the time, "The sale of tobacco products is inconsistent with our purpose."[18] Yes, it is. It makes it hard to believe that competitor Walgreens still sold tobacco products as of early 2022.

DEBRIEF

Today's customers make it clear they want to do business with organizations that reflect their own beliefs. To review, my recommendations on how to start building reputation capital are:

- prioritize culture

- reflect on feedback

- become a thought leader

- cultivate an online audience

- create content

- exercise corporate citizenship

- choose a highest value

Not *every* organization that adopts these principles will necessarily be recognized as outstanding among its peers. Conversely, some brands that ignore (or seemingly ignore) many of these best practices continue to thrive.

Certain businesses, including those in highly regulated industries—like airlines, professional sports leagues, energy companies, cable television, and, yes, social media—exist in markets where there's limited competition. Consumers have only so many choices when it comes to watching a professional football game, heating their home with natural gas, or selecting a cable provider.

Case in point: Facebook reported 2.89 billion monthly active users in the second quarter of 2021.[19] It's become ubiquitous in how we get news—36 percent of US adults say they regularly get news on the platform[20]—and how businesses advertise—Facebook's domestic ad revenue accounted for a 23.8 percent share of the United States' total digital ad spending in 2021.[21] Even with its pattern of betraying the public trust, Facebook continues to be wildly profitable. All the complaints and gnashing of teeth haven't slowed the social network's exponential growth or put a significant dent in its stock price.

And yet, beginning in late 2021, the toll of facing one crisis after another appeared to be chipping away at the social network's profitability. Consider:

- Facebook is reportedly now paying a "brand tax" to tech workers who are afraid that working at the company could jeopardize their future job prospects.[22] As a result, 2022 expenses at the company were projected to jump as high as $97 billion from $70 billion.[23]

- In January 2022, a federal judge allowed the Federal Trade Commission's effort to break up Facebook to proceed in the courts. The FTC wants to reverse Facebook's acquisitions of Instagram and WhatsApp, arguing the social media giant represents a monopoly.[24]

- In February 2022, Facebook set the record for the largest one-day value drop in stock market history, losing more than $232 billion after it reported weaker-than-expected first-quarter revenue.[25]

- All social media platforms face significant risk due to the possible reform of Section 230 of the Communications Decency Act, the law that protects these companies from being held legally liable for user content.

Are the years of missteps by the company now known as Meta finally hitting home? We'll see. It reinforces the notion, however, that sustainable success is most assured when brands make decisions aligned not just with profit but also with the greater good.

2

THE BEST-MANAGED CRISES (ARE THE ONES YOU'VE NEVER HEARD OF)

CRISIS COMMUNICATIONS IS, essentially, a defensive discipline falling under the practice of public relations. Although PR and crisis work share some strategies and tactics, they could not be more different in the range of outcomes that constitute a success or failure.

In traditional public relations, the optimal result is often securing a front-page placement or, perhaps, a coveted spot on the opinion page of a major newspaper. However, when our firm is retained by clients anticipating or experiencing a crisis, the best possible outcome is that the issue never becomes public or appears in the press. While there's the well-worn cliché of a corporate boss calling in their communications chief and demanding they "kill" or "squash" a story, in reality, that can't happen without good reason.

GETTING AHEAD OF THE PROBLEM

On our first call with a client, I'll ask several pointed questions to assess the severity and time sensitivity of the issue along with the potential audiences we'll need to communicate with. That way, we can help formulate a holistic response strategy that includes the necessary materials with the appropriate sense of urgency.

Here are some suggestions of how to keep the lid on a brewing reputational threat.

Ask Yourself, "Is It a Threat or a Crisis?"

Some situations might be labeled a crisis within an organization but won't be considered newsworthy by a reporter. What makes for good watercooler talk or office gossip is often viewed by the press as inside-baseball. I've witnessed, time and again, the groupthink that can take hold inside an organization and how it can instill, among leadership, a skewed perception of the issue's importance among external audiences.

Past client issues and crises I've managed that didn't result in media coverage include staff layoffs, leadership changes, the discontinuation of popular programs, and litigation by former employees against the organization. Reporters may not have been aware of the situation, but in most cases, they were and didn't find the facts compelling enough to share with their readers, viewers, or listeners.

Although one should always be *prepared* to communicate, there will be instances in which proactively sharing information won't be the right move. If you're under no legal or ethical obligation, never assume you should automatically disclose bad news. Sharing information that your stakeholders would likely never hear about otherwise is rarely the right call. Plus, it could eat up a significant amount of time your executive team could spend elsewhere.

Set the Record Straight

Journalists often receive inaccurate or incomplete information, especially when a source has an ax to grind. Perhaps it's a disgruntled former employee who felt mistreated on the way out the door. Maybe it's a neighborhood group opposed to an extensive real estate development, fearful of what the extra traffic could mean for the surrounding streets. Regardless, individuals and groups reaching out to reporters are often not impartial; they have an agenda.

When I first connect with a reporter on the phone on my client's behalf, I request our conversations be *off the record*, which the Associated Press defines as a conversation in which the "the information cannot be used for publication."[1] Some journalists will decline, preferring all conversations to be *on the record* and thus quotable. That typically makes for a short call. Moving forward, I'll limit our communication to email or text, where I can keep our conversation brief and to the point, mindful that anything I say could end up being quoted in the final story.

Still, I've found most reporters *are* willing to engage in a conversation in which nothing discussed is reportable or attributable. Such an arrangement can prove valuable for both sides. First, it creates an environment with the leeway to speak freely and provide additional context, which the reporter will appreciate. Second, the spokesperson or I won't have to be concerned about misspeaking and being quoted.

Because a reporter can take information you provide *off the record* and follow up with other sources *on the record*, there's an incentive to take what you tell them seriously. Vice versa, there are times they'll get a tip from a source looking to disparage your client that's provided *off the record*. In that case, it's the journalist's responsibility to corroborate or confirm that account of the incident or issue *on the record*. Not being able to do so makes it virtually impossible for them to then write their story.

Sometimes the details we negotiate with a journalist are objective (which facts to include) and sometimes they're subjective (whose opinion or account the reporter gives more credence to). Suppose a reporter is writing a story and, realistically, there's nothing we can do to persuade them otherwise. In that case, we work as hard as we can to ensure our client receives a fair shake and prominent positioning in the story.

In the rare instance where I truly believe the reporter is biased or editorializing in what's supposed to be a straight news story, I'll respectfully ask to speak with their editor. Some of my appeals have resulted in favorable edits for my client, others have not. Still, even a minor victory is worth it if it means having some additional context included or there's a slight change to a headline that takes some of the sting out of a critical piece.

Be Proactive

While crisis communications is primarily reactionary in nature, there are times when playing offense will be called for. Instead of sitting back and waiting for more negative developments, consider what opportunities exist to drive the storyline.

Going on the offensive can help blunt and diminish the bad news you're expecting. Certainly, this can be effective online, where the most effective strategy to drive down negative search engine results is to organically create positive content such as news, blogs, and the like, so it ranks higher.

It might not be conventional thinking to consider a genuine branding opportunity when a crisis is swirling. But if the circumstances are right, there may well be opportunities to bring about a fresh round of positive news coverage. Examples include a large charitable donation or a new product rollout.

In late 2021, after claims of allowing a culture of sexual harassment at the video game giant Activision, longtime CEO Bobby Kotick slashed his salary (his 2020 pay package totaled $154.6 million), pledged a "new zero-tolerance harassment policy," and promised to increase the percentage of women and nonbinary people in the workforce by 50 percent.[2]

Although Kotick's actions were admirable, some employees and investors still called for his resignation after a subsequent *Wall Street Journal* exposé, which claimed the CEO knew of sexual misconduct allegations across the organization, and didn't report them to the company's board of directors.[3] As of this writing, Kotick has reportedly told senior managers he would consider leaving the company if he can't quickly fix its culture problems.[4]

Prevent the Spread of Mis/Disinformation

The rise of misinformation (inaccurate, but the spreader *believes* it's true) and disinformation (inaccurate and manufactured with the *intent* to spread lies) is an increasingly significant threat to reputation capital. Social media only fuels this fake news fire.

Consider a 2018 study by the Massachusetts Institute of Technology, which found that fake news on Twitter travels six times faster than factual news.[5] Social media algorithms, which aid the rapid dissemination of false news, are designed to enrage and engage users so they remain on the channels longer. On top of this, those maliciously spreading lies always seem to be several steps ahead of those racing to produce tools that can help us distinguish between real and fake content.

Disinformation is rapidly becoming more sophisticated and easier to create. Take so-called deepfake videos, where advanced technology is used to "paste" someone's face on another person's body or make it appear and sound as if someone said something they did not.

Identifying this content early and taking proactive measures to mitigate the potential damage is essential. Simply tracking mainstream social media is no longer sufficient. With a substantial amount of false information originating on the internet's fringes or the dark web, many prominent brands require sophisticated early-detection devices and services. Monitoring software that scans sites and reads content can flag threats not long after they appear. This helps the user get ahead of false information, tamp down lies, and define the narrative with accurate information.

Still, the best way for a brand to combat mis/disinformation is consistently living exemplary values, making those values known, and ensuring stakeholders understand where it comes down on issues important to the community, as discussed in the previous chapter.

Make Connections

If you have a relationship you know you'll need to count on during a potential crisis, invest in it early. Perhaps it's a regulator, the mayor's office, or a college administrator. Whoever it might be, it always helps if you've established a connection and familiarity with those who could be of assistance or who might be asking hard questions when the going gets tough.

For example, a client who owns and operates office buildings across the country regularly holds crisis drills. Sitting around a large table, participants verbally respond to a hypothetical crisis (announced by a moderator) with the actions they would take in a real-life emergency. This client invites local police and fire departments and special tactical response teams to the crisis exercise to sit alongside tenant representatives as well as the building's security staff, maintenance, and food service workers. We'll address these "tabletop" exercises in greater detail in chapter 7.

In a scenario in which first responders are required, having a trusted and open line of communication can benefit both parties. Consider sharing your crisis response and communications plans with local authorities or a security consultant to solicit feedback and ensure your preparations reflect industry best practices.

By fostering these strong relationships, those you may need to deal with when tensions are running high will be able to act more efficiently and may be more likely to do you a favor when you need it most.

COMPOUNDING A CRISIS

As the opening quote from billionaire investor and philanthropist Warren Buffett suggests, you can do everything right to build a flawless reputation over years of hard work, only to lose that goodwill in the blink of an eye. That's why at the same time you're making deposits to accumulate reputation capital, you should be identifying and addressing your brand's vulnerabilities. These might include:

- outdated cybersecurity

- supply chains that rely on single sourcing

- a senior executive with a history of sexual harassment or domestic violence

- a facility that is not up to the latest fire codes

Even if you've identified and resolved any of these vulnerabilities, a botched or inadequate response could ensure that an issue remains in the headlines, to the detriment of your reputation capital, longer than it needs to. Whether those at the helm are motivated by ego or truly do not appreciate the likely implications of their actions, a mismanaged response typically includes one or more of the following actions.

They Can't Bring Themselves to Apologize

Accepting responsibility won't get the job done in many scenarios unless there is a clear and forthright apology. This mea culpa is the signal, recognition, and acknowledgment many aggrieved parties desire most. Saying "I'm sorry" can have a powerful, even medicinal, effect, like a salve that helps soothe. An apology can facilitate reconciliation. It might even persuade individuals to drop a lawsuit and move on with their lives by draining some emotional reasons—such as resentment or a desire to punish—for pursuing a claim.

"The apology fulfills some of the goals that triggered the suit, such as a need for respect, to assign responsibility and to get a sense that what happened won't happen again," according to the *Michigan Law Review* study *Apologies and Legal Settlement: An Empirical Examination.*[6] It goes on to report, "So receiving an apology can reduce financial aspirations and make it possible for parties to enter into discussions about settlement."

Such a case took place in 2009, when the actor James Woods sued a Rhode Island Hospital for the death of his brother Michael on behalf of Michael's children. But when the hospital's CEO and president apologized, saying, "I am so sorry," it ended Woods's determination not to settle.[7] He said that it "made discussion possible in a case where I had no interest in settlement and was absolutely certain of victory," adding that he "did agree that [the hospital's] apology was genuine and not a ploy."[8]

Two of the greatest innovators of our age illustrate the PR blowback that can ensue when brands refuse to apologize for an incident or issue they should take responsibility for:

- When Apple released the iPhone 4 in 2010, customers complained about signal issues. Instead of owning the faulty antenna problem, Apple essentially blamed the user in its official statement, which included:

    Gripping any phone will result in some attenuation of its antenna performance, with certain places being worse than others depending on the placement of the antennas. This is a fact of life for every wireless phone.[9]

    The late Steve Jobs dismissed the difficulty experienced by his customers as a non-issue.[10] In the end, Apple conceded that the iPhone 4's reception problem resulted from a hardware flaw and eventually settled a class-action lawsuit over the matter.

- Following the 2016 death of a Florida man when Tesla's autopilot system didn't detect a truck crossing the highway, Elon Musk used social and traditional media to defend the safety of the autopilot system. The company posted blogs about the accident and referred to the young man's death as a "statistical inevitability."[11]

Skirting accountability, especially when lives are lost, will be viewed negatively unless forces are genuinely beyond the brand's control.

However, there are instances when apologizing for *wrongdoing* might not be the appropriate response. Remember, saying "I am sorry" without explaining what you are sorry *for* can be easily misinterpreted as accepting guilt or responsibility. The inference, of course, is that you must have done something wrong. That's why explaining what you are sorry *for* in detail is essential to limiting legal exposure. When the situation calls for it, apologies should be focused on empathy or sympathy for the other's pain and suffering. For instance:

- When a factory worker is injured in an accident, management finds ways to support the team member and apologizes for the hardship they've had to endure. That doesn't necessarily mean accepting responsibility for the accident itself.

- When an employee claims they're a victim of workplace harassment, management apologizes to the individual for having experienced a situation in which they felt disrespected and threatened. Perhaps they even end up suspending or terminating the alleged perpetrator. Still, this doesn't mean accepting responsibility for an environment that tolerates this behavior.

These are just two examples of projecting humility while balancing legal considerations as well as today's expectation that brands will not discount the suffering of others. Within the apology, it might also be appropriate for leadership to communicate its priorities (e.g., creating a safe and healthy work environment) and to do all it can to address the problem sufficiently and put safeguards or processes in place to prevent a reoccurrence.

They Issue a "No Comment"

We've all read or heard those two words enough times to associate a negative connotation with them every time they're uttered by someone facing a personal or professional crisis. A "no comment" *is* a comment in the eyes of the public. It communicates a bunker mentality, a sense that the individual or organization is either unprepared or can't be bothered to stand up for itself. When you're watching the news and a business executive utters "no comment" to a reporter's rapid-fire questions, what do you think? I imagine it's that they might as well be saying "I'm guilty," "none of your business," or "I wish you'd just go away and leave me alone."

Brands in crisis might be entitled to stonewall the press in hot pursuit of a story, but the mere appearance of doing so will begin to chip away at its reputation. No matter how many great reviews or how much charitable giving is in its past, a "no comment" when an organization is under the microscope conveys an unacceptable lack of transparency and a belligerent attitude. Like pleading the Fifth, it's perfectly legal to do so, but it casts a bad light.

There's *always* something else that can be said, such as:

- *I'm not aware of the situation you're asking about, but let me look into it.*

- *I'm not prepared to issue a statement right now, but if you give me your contact information I will let you know as soon as I am.*

Even if a spokesperson follows up with a written statement, it's giving the reporter (and thus the public) *something* that will make the brand look less afraid of commenting on the issue. Those unwilling to even offer a response during the tough times shouldn't expect that same reporter to then cover them in the good times.

They Lash Out

When a leader views the unwanted attention brought on by an organizational crisis as a *personal* attack, they often lash out in response. That lack of poise and awareness typically damages an individual's credibility. Best case, they appear thin-skinned and undisciplined. Worse case, the public perceives them as unprofessional and unhinged.

When a CEO's first instinct may be to retaliate or to let an individual or reporter know that some high-powered corporate attorneys will hold them accountable, it rarely has the desired effect. In fact, it signals to the public that they've struck a nerve and are onto something. Like issuing a "no comment," it's letting everyone know that you've something to hide.

In February 2017, a dashboard camera or "dash cam" captured former Uber CEO Travis Kalanick in the back of a car driven by an Uber driver, arguing about falling fares. The exchange compounded questions about Kalanick's ability to lead due to several controversies at the time involving him and the leading brand in ridesharing. Bloomberg's coverage of the incident included speculation that "Kalanick's pugnacious personality and short temper . . . may cause some investors to question whether he has the disposition to lead a $69 billion company."[12] By June of the same year, he was forced to step down as CEO.

Kalanick would've been better off listening and taking the criticism to heart, as the CEO of Whole Foods did in the example presented earlier. It's never a smart move for a leader to retaliate or seek revenge for short-term satisfaction.

"SHUT UP. HIRE A PUBLIC RELATIONS CONSULTANT."

The first big story I covered for ABC News was the Crandall Canyon Mine collapse. For a week in August 2007, my colleagues and I worked out of a Winnebago-style motor home in the rugged mountains of Utah, writing and producing stories around the clock on what was unfolding approximately fifteen hundred feet underground. In addition to the devastating and heartbreaking loss of the life, what I recall most vividly was the combative nature of the mine's owner, the late Robert Murray.

In a story from August 8 of that year, headlined "Murray's Meltdown," the *Salt Lake Tribune* cited the Murray Energy CEO's "disjointed, rambling" appearance at a press conference, where he attacked the media, union organizers, and environmentalists and blamed an earthquake for the collapse.[13] In an opinion piece after the press conference, *Tribune* columnist Rebecca Walsh blasted Murray, leaving little room for interpretation: "Shut up. Hire a public relations consultant. And soon."[14]

Nine people lost their lives in the initial collapse and subsequent rescue attempt. When a CEO communicates in the wake of such a tragedy, their words should soothe and convey empathy. A leader should never put themselves and their ego above the memory of those who've been lost. Doing so communicates disrespect and a perverse set of priorities when the loved ones of those lost are suffering and still in mourning.

They Blame Others or Portray Themselves as the Victim

This is a strategy I advise against unless it's genuinely (and I mean *genuinely*) justified. Typically, it comes off as tone-deaf and insulting to the aggrieved party or the public at large. Blaming others is especially egregious in a David and Goliath struggle, such as when a publicly traded company is perceived as picking on a single customer. Engaging in this "Woe is me!" strategy often results in the spokesperson and the organization they represent appearing pompous, entitled, and condescending.

For example, in 2015, Chipotle Mexican Grill faced an outbreak of *E. coli* that sickened 55 customers across eleven states and forced the chain to temporarily close some of its locations.[15] As if that wasn't enough of a PR crisis, two months later, up to 140 people fell ill from a norovirus outbreak linked to a Chipotle in Boston. It was a significant reputational hit for a brand that prided itself on fresh ingredients and sustainable practices. The company's stock price fell 24 percent.[16]

To make matters worse, Chipotle co-CEO Monty Moran told Wall Street analysts:

> *Because the media likes to write sensational headlines, we'll probably see when somebody sneezes that they're going to say, "Ah, it's E. coli from Chipotle" for a little bit of time. And so that's unfortunate.*[17]

In damage-control mode, Chipotle founder Steve Ells went on national television the next day. He began with an apology and then articulated his commitment, "The procedures we're putting in place today are so above industry norms that we are going to be the safest place to eat."[18] The next day, Chipotle's stock jumped 5 percent.[19] The belief that a strategy of blaming others for a brand's troubles will have negative repercussions is backed up by a 2015 study from the University of Missouri–Columbia, which found companies typically benefit when they publicly accept blame for poor performance:

Companies that accepted blame and had a plan to address their problems stopped the decline in their share prices after their announcement, but those companies that blamed others continued to experience falling share prices for the entire year following their public explanation.[20]

Crisis communicators must think long and hard about what the public will and won't find plausible. At these times, being able to confer with outside consultants removed from the echo chamber of your organization can prove especially valuable. Even if they're attorneys or PR professionals you've had a long-term partnership with, they still bring a third-party perspective. Their point of view is closer to how the public might interpret a set of facts than someone on the inside.

My colleagues and I often offer counsel, in writing, to internal communications staff, who then pass on recommendations to the higher-ups. It's not uncommon, however, for my counterpart to ask that I provide my thoughts directly to the CEO. They know, especially at a moment of crisis, that the perspective of an outsider is likely to make a more significant impression than feedback from those the CEO hears from day in, day out.

BLAMING THE PRESS: NOT A STRATEGY

One cautionary tale about blaming others for your troubles emerged from the Sony Pictures Entertainment email hack of 2014. The breach, by a terrorist group believed to be connected to North Korea, occurred just as the movie studio was about to release the political satire *The Interview*. The film was about a CIA plot to assassinate North Korean dictator Kim Jong Un.

The leaked communications between the studio's executives exposed intellectual property in addition to embarrassing conversations around race, gender, and pay inequality. In response to the media coverage, Sony's lawyer sent a threatening letter to the press, calling the leaked material "stolen information" and demanding that they notify Sony if they were in possession of this material AND that they delete it immediately.[21]

The letter went on to say,

If you do not comply with this request, and the Stolen Informa-tion is used or disseminated by you in any manner, SPE [Sony Pictures Entertainment] will have no choice but to hold you responsible for any damage or loss arising from such use or dissemination by you.[22]

Subsequent media coverage portrayed Sony's legal team as a paper tiger, threatening action they were powerless to enforce. On top of that, the reporting didn't stop. The press argued that so long as they didn't play any part in obtaining the hacked emails, they had every right to report on them if they were deemed newsworthy.

Whether Sony had a legal case or not, publicly attacking the press was never going to make it a sympathetic figure in the eyes of the public. It's a strategy my colleagues and I advise against unless the coverage is truly inaccurate and accuses a brand of things for which it bears no responsibility. Instead, Sony compounded the dam-age, making the embarrassed studio executives appear bitter and thin-skinned.

They Consider Only the Legal Consequences

With the omnipresence of 24-hour media, we're bombarded by an unre-lenting stream of news and information. Citizen journalists, armed with smartphones, have the ability to post still images and video on social media with no editorial oversight. It's in this environment that expec-tations around corporate transparency and accountability are at an all-time high.

As a result, the partnership between legal and public relations profes-sionals is vital, perhaps in a way never before imagined, to ensure their strategies are aligned. We each play a distinct role but share the common goal of protecting our client.

One reason to consider having both perspectives at the table from the outset boils down to language. When it comes to attorneys, the necessity of linguistic precision has been described this way:

In the study of law, language has great importance; cases turn on
the meaning that judges ascribe to words, and lawyers must use
the right words to effectuate the wishes of their clients . . . you're
expected to use them with precision. Substituting one for another
can result in serious errors and misunderstandings.[23]

While that calculated language is necessary in a court of law, the PR
professional specializes in a more colloquial style of communication.
Legal language isn't designed to be *sensitive*, while language drafted by
a PR professional and intended for public consumption is. PR pros are
skilled at taking complex speech or jargon, distilling its key messages,
and converting those messages into easily digestible information for a
mass audience or key stakeholder group.

Aside from the debate over language, the back and forth between PR
and legal takes place over strategy: *how much* of an issue we can divulge
in a public statement. For instance, there are strict privacy laws when it
comes to sharing information about an employee, a medical patient, or
a student. If that person is hurling accusations against one of our clients
in the press, defending that organization can be akin to boxing with one
arm tied behind your back.

When the accuser makes derogatory statements about your client
and a reporter asks for a response, the typical "all employee/patient/
student matters are confidential" won't always cut it. Many attorneys
today understand that some circumstances require making exceptions
to protocols around privacy and disclosure.

In especially high-profile cases, attorneys have asked my colleagues
and me to review court filings with a fine-tooth comb. This attention to
detail ensures the documents don't contain language that could trip up
the client if the press uses them as source material for a story, as they
often do.

As we saw in the case of Sony Entertainment, such caution should
also be weighed with cease-and-desist letters, which have traditionally
included paragraphs of punitive legal language. These communications,

traded between attorneys representing two warring factions, were rarely the subject of significant media attention or public ire. But thanks to social media, many infamous examples of cease-and-desist letters have been widely criticized and mocked, and they're increasingly a part of traditional media coverage.

That's why we recommend that clients and their lawyers view these communications as a potential PR opportunity rather than a strictly legal action. Instead of filing a cease-and-desist letter with threatening legalese only, we suggest softening the tone. That way, if it's leaked or otherwise shared publicly, it will depict a thoughtful and understandable request as opposed to a tirade intended to intimidate. While the latter might help ensure an airtight legal strategy, it can easily come back to bite a brand, portraying it as brusque and heavy-handed.

The opposite is also true. If we're crafting a media holding statement or community letter, we draft with the knowledge that such documents could also be entered into evidence in any subsequent litigation. That's why we always make sure legal counsel reviews all public messaging. While they might push for a more conservative approach, we can typically find common ground to construct the most effective defense for our mutual client.

The number of instances in which a high-profile brand considered *only* the legal ramifications of a reputational threat are too many to list. One glaring instance was the response to a crisis that consumed United Airlines for months. It's such a textbook case of what *not* to do that I've dedicated an entire case study in this book to review the incident in detail and to analyze the many missteps that kept this story in the headlines significantly longer than it needed to be.

They Take Too Long to Respond or Disclose

When your reputation is on the line, you would think a quick response would be a natural reaction, practically hardwired in our DNA. But *analysis paralysis* is real, and it can have a brand playing catchup when the media is churning out stories and chatter about the issue is trending or going viral on social media. The same goes for discovering an issue that will impact your community but not sharing need-to-know information fast enough.

Although your instinct may be to wait until the full scope of a crisis or the total amount of damage is known before going public, my advice is to be up-front as soon as possible and not wait the weeks or longer required to conduct a comprehensive investigation. Promptly sharing information with your key constituents communicates that they matter.

Although it might be painful to provide continuous updates—knowing that with each communication you're potentially reporting a more significant crisis—transparency is paramount. Nothing depletes reputation capital faster than the perception that you're withholding important information your community deserves to know.

THE "TOO LITTLE, TOO LATE" RESPONSE

A cautionary tale of how not to respond publicly to a cyberattack began in July 2005. This is when, over the next year and a half, hackers would end up stealing more than 45.7 million credit and debit card numbers from the TJX Companies, the owner of major retail brands including T.J. Maxx, Marshalls, and HomeGoods.[24]

TJX discovered the breach in December 2006, yet it was kept private until mid-January 2007. A March 2007 story in CSO Online reported, "That gave the company time to secure its systems and law enforcement time to investigate. But to many in the public, it looked like a retailer sitting on bad PR until after the important holiday season."[25] Even today, it's still cited as one of the most poorly managed breaches because of how it was communicated.

Today's consumers expect quick notification and a company's full transparency around how the breach occurred, what data was exposed or vulnerable, how long the incident lasted, and what's being done to shore up cybersecurity to prevent a repeat hack. Brands should make information readily available on their website or in an email. Most critical, consumers expect live human beings who can answer questions in real time over the phone or live chat.

While proactive outreach to the media isn't required (or recommended) in the wake of a breach, reporters will learn of it soon enough if brands are communicating with those directly impacted. Like bridge or stop-gap statements, demonstrating transparency while not having all the facts can be facilitated through messages that frame information in ways that it never has to be walked back. These statements should include phrases such as:

"What we know at this time is . . . "

"We have found no evidence of . . . "

"What we've learned so far . . . "

Expectations of how brands communicate in the wake of a cyberattack have evolved significantly over the past two decades. Ensure your crisis plan includes the response steps necessary should your organization face this increasingly common breach of confidence.

KNOWING WHEN *NOT* TO APOLOGIZE

I've described how certain communications will be received positively only if they include a forthright and heart-felt apology. I've also shared examples such as the iPhone 4 "Antennagate" scandal where saying, "I'm sorry" was the obvious and necessary move, only certain leaders just couldn't bring themselves to do so.

Admittedly, whether or not to apologize is not always an easy choice. It might seem like the fast and most direct way out of a trouble, but it's also evolved into a crutch of sorts or, as *Vox* called it, "a safety blanket for brands mindful of damage control."[26]

In reality, an apology won't always be appropriate or necessary. Over-apologizing or apologizing for minor issues can make a leader and the brand appear weak and defensive. Here are some scenarios when saying "I'm sorry" might not be the right call.

When No One Would've Otherwise Noticed

Would stakeholders even hear about the issue if you didn't offer a public apology? Remember, just your brand is getting significant engagement on Twitter about a topic doesn't mean it embodies the beliefs of your entire customer base. The voices on social media tend to be the most extreme, so consider other sources and data before concluding that your community is clamoring for an apology.

Has the issue gained traction, or is it likely to blow over in 48 hours? According to the American Marketing Association, "the trick is to determine whether the error is egregious enough for a proactive apology or if the act of addressing the mistake does more harm than good."[27]

When an Offense Is Perceived, Not Real

Issuing a one-on-one apology for poor customer service is one thing, but not everyone's interpretation of a larger issue will be an accurate representation of what occurred. Now that social media provides every consumer with a bullhorn to criticize or congratulate, many brands are quick to fall on their sword to tamp down any negative noise rather than to stand on principle and rely on their ample reputation capital.

Of course, perception can often be reality. So how does a brand know if it's dealing with a situation that requires an apology? This is where measuring the engagement of social media posts can help, along with a closer look at *who* has taken offense. If it's a Twitter "mob" not likely to include your customers or other key stakeholders, that *could* be an indication that an apology isn't necessary.

PRESSURED INTO AN APOLOGY

In 2017, Dove apologized after screenshots of its latest campaign incited a massive backlash. The images, taken from a GIF and part of an ad for body wash, depicted a Black woman removing her top to reveal a White woman. The beauty brand was quickly accused of racism because of the screenshots, which many took to mean that white skin was somehow "cleaner." In fact, the full-length ad, which many did not get to see, included five women of different ethnicities, each morphing into the next. Dove's message: the company celebrates diversity, and its products are for all women.

Feeling the heat, Dove pulled the GIF from its Facebook page and tweeted that it "missed the mark in representing women of color thoughtfully." Even so, its apology—"we deeply regret the offense it caused"—wasn't enough for most of the nearly seven thousand users who commented.[28] Most were critical and called for a boycott of Dove's products.

Dove had been well respected on the issue of diversity, leveraging well-established initiatives like its Real Beauty Campaign and Self-Esteem Project.[29] The Unilever-owned brand has long encouraged women to embrace their physical appearance.

The model of Nigerian descent who appeared in the ad insisted, "I don't feel it was racist," during an interview with the BBC. "It wasn't even the full ad that people had issue with. Because of this, a different narrative has been presented."[30]

Dove, at worst, was guilty of choosing the wrong images for its Facebook page. The brand said it was "re-evaluating our internal processes for creating and approving content to prevent us making this type of mistake in the future."[31]

Dove could have had the courage of its convictions, explained that the GIF did not accurately represent the larger campaign, and defended its creative vision in a statement such as: All women are beautiful, and we didn't believe the order in which they appeared in the ad was critical to that message, but we understand how the image was misinterpreted.

A brand that's done so much to raise awareness and elevate the conversation about self-esteem has earned the benefit of the doubt. Talking about race and body image is not a safe space for any brand. Yet Dove had the reputation capital to address, in a genuine way, the insecurities with which many of us, both women and men, struggle.

When Not Enough Time Has Passed

When it comes to pure reputational crises (where public safety hasn't already been compromised or isn't at risk), too quick of a response might come off as knee-jerk and insincere. Allowing a little bit of time to pass can be interpreted as the brand thoughtfully weighing the situation and deciding on the best way to respond.

Even though template language should be ready to go in the crisis plan (to be discussed in chapter 5), that doesn't mean it should be issued or posted on social media as quickly as it can be customized for a specific situation. This might be perceived as merely going through the motions without enough serious consideration. Too many apologies from one brand are akin to the boy who cried wolf, making it unclear whether the apology is meaningful or not.

When It's a Half Apology

This starts with "I'm sorry" and includes a "but" before transitioning to another message altogether. It's an attempt to have it both ways, expressing contrition while, at the same time, attaching caveats. For instance, the circumstances were out of the brand's control, this doesn't usually happen, or someone else was partially to blame.

If the word *but* is used in a statement intended to make amends, it typically renders everything that comes before, including the actual apology, inconsequential in the eyes of the reader. In such a case, why make an apology at all?

DEBRIEF

Some threats or crises will make news when information leaks occur, a disgruntled stakeholder tips off a reporter, or public disclosure is mandated by law. However, plenty of times it's how leaders manage (or don't manage) a threat that determines whether a situation stays under wraps. The suggestions offered in this chapter include:

- asking yourself, "Is it a threat or a crisis?"

- getting real with reporters to provide context

- being proactive, not just reactive, when possible

- preventing the spread of mis/disinformation

- making connections with those who could help during an actual crisis

It's not uncommon for our firm to hear from a business *after* their initial crisis response was a swing and a miss. Perhaps it was due to complacency, insensitivity, or simply misreading the situation. Regardless, only when it failed did they realize they needed outside help.

Much like the physician's guiding maxim "Do no harm," an inadequate response will compound an already bad situation. Never do *anything* that would attract additional negative attention about you or your organization, especially when already under a microscope. As discussed, the following missteps by leadership can make matters worse:

- They can't bring themselves to apologize.

- They issue a "no comment."

- They lash out.

- They blame others or portray themselves as the victim.

- They consider only the legal consequences.

- They take too long to respond or disclose.

While there are crises that literally will not pass until the catharsis of an apology occurs, there are other times when leaders will be judged as weak and lacking a backbone if the public believes they've caved too easily. Among the times *not* to apologize are:

- when no one would've otherwise noticed

- when an offense is perceived, not real

- when not enough time has passed

- when it's a half apology

Corporate apologies can be powerful moments if delivered for the right reasons and at the right time. They demonstrate humility and vulnerability. Let the situation dictate whether one is truly necessary.

Like the expression "It's not the crime, it's the cover-up," the same could be said for managing a reputational threat, scandal, or emergency: it's not the crisis, it's the response. Any organization can face an issue at any time. Along with how the brand was perceived beforehand, how it responds at the moment of truth determines whether that issue is contained or whether it spirals out of control.

3

THE TEN (CRISIS) COMMANDMENTS

NO TWO CRISES ARE THE SAME. Even if the transgression, accident, or mishap is similar to others, there are always variants, such as the context in which the crisis is occurring, the players who are at its center, or the stakeholders who are impacted the most.

What's the brand's reputation capital at the outset of the crisis? Has it been involved in previous controversies, or is its record squeaky clean? Is it genuinely philanthropic or perceived as merely self-serving? What do employees, past and present, say about working there? While a particular response might prove effective for one organization during a crisis, the same response might fail spectacularly if rolled out in a scenario in which the variables differ only slightly.

While a one-size-fits-all approach is never appropriate, there are some hard and fast rules when planning for or responding to a crisis. Consider these ten universal truths, or "commandments," when strategizing.

1. Plan Ahead

One crisis survey co-conducted in late 2019 found that just 62 percent of companies reported having crisis plans they're familiar with.[1] In addition, the survey revealed that few companies prepare by consistently running practice drills as if they were responding to a real threat.

As I said earlier, it's inexcusable for any company to not have a crisis response infrastructure in place. Don't be lulled into a false sense of security: no one and no brand is immune. Wishing a crisis away won't do the trick; an effective response requires forward thinking and detailed planning. Some insurance carriers may even provide discounted rates to clients with a crisis management plan in place or will reimburse fees for outside consultants when dealing with an urgent matter.

As I'll expound upon in chapter 5, any responsible organization should have a written plan with contact information, response protocols, media procedures, and ready-to-go templated language that can be quickly customized with details.

In formulating a plan, a first step should be evaluating an organization's vulnerabilities and pinpointing issues that have near- or long-term potential to escalate into a full-blown crisis. Then, focus on those scenarios and strategize how to immediately address each issue before it becomes a bona fide reputational risk. Part of planning ahead means knowing when to look outside your organization for expertise that may not exist in-house.

2. Inform and Educate

If supporters sense that a brand is trying to exploit a crisis to sell them more services or products, its efforts will be perceived as foolish and inappropriate. During an emergency, it's paramount that an organization establish itself as *the* credible source for reliable information.

Never was this function of crisis communications more critical than during the early days of the COVID-19 pandemic. Employees, residents, students, patients, and other stakeholders were looking for facts and guidance during a confusing, uncertain, and scary time.

Below is a communication we drafted on behalf of a client for residents of an apartment building.

Dear Residents,

As of Wednesday, the mayor has issued a stay-at-home order effective Friday, March 27, at 12:01 a.m. through Friday, April 10, to help slow the spread of COVID-19, with the exception of certain essential activities and work outlined in the order.

Under these most recent municipal guidelines, residential operations are considered essential, so we will continue to have current management and maintenance staff on-site. However, we are no longer conducting face-to-face business, and residents should call the office for assistance at the number indicated below or utilize our resident portal if you need to contact the office. As a reminder, all amenity spaces including the gym remain closed, and we are only processing emergency work orders until further notice.

Your safety and well-being are our first priority, and we ask that you please continue to practice guidelines as recommended by the Centers for Disease Control and Prevention (CDC) during this time at home, and social distancing. Should you have any flu-like symptoms or test positive for COVID-19, please contact the office to let us know.

We are closely monitoring information from the city and the state, the CDC, and the World Health Organization and will continue to keep you updated as the situation evolves.
Thank you.

Our client understood that, in addition to letting residents know that in-person meetings were on hold and common spaces would be closed until restrictions were lifted, providing useful information would reassure community members and might help prevent the spread of the virus.

3. Be Accountable

Anyone can accept the compliments readily available during the good times, but character is truly defined during the tough ones. This is when an organization can prove itself genuinely worthy of the loyal following it's built through years of hard work.

For example, if you run an e-commerce site and a product is recalled due to safety issues, do what you can to be part of the solution. Sure, your site isn't responsible for the supply chain issues that led to the recall, but you're one of the public faces of the product. Therefore, you should accept some of the responsibility in supporting consumers by answering questions and helping to mitigate the situation.

Typically, the fork in the road for many brands is deciding whether or not to accept responsibility for a negative issue or event. The initial rationale for *not* taking responsibility tends to be, "If I explain my side of what occurred and why, then others will see it my way and understand that I'm not responsible." Of course, each situation must be assessed on its own merits, but that approach rarely works. In this book's two case studies, you'll see what happens when a CEO accepts responsibility from the outset and what happens when they don't.

4. Respond Rapidly

If a brand takes accountability, but only after weeks of evading blame, it'll likely suffer the same reputational hit as if it never did. When disaster strikes, the default mode should be to move as quickly as possible. If the emergency occurs on a Friday afternoon, waiting until Monday morning to respond won't cut it. Assemble decision makers immediately to gather the facts, assess the potential fallout, and strategize a response.

A lackadaisical response could leave your organization vulnerable and unable to muster the most effective response. It puts you behind the eight ball when driving the narrative and conveying your side of the story. I've never received a media inquiry from a reporter during a client crisis who told me, "If you could get back to me next week, that would be great." Instead, it's typically, "We're filing a story in an hour or two."

Suppose you're facing a problem, and a reporter reaches out for an initial response. Taking the opportunity to issue a written statement or provide an actual interview is essential. Why? Every subsequent story could cite or pull a quote from the first story published. So if you decline to comment for that initial piece of reporting or can't make the reporter's deadline, the characterization risks being repeated in multiple stories and shared an infinite number of times across social media. You'll then have to spend an unnecessary and inordinate amount of time playing catchup, proactively reaching out to those outlets, and asking them to update their stories with your response. Instead, you could be managing the actual crisis as opposed to putting out unnecessary fires.

ONE CRISIS, MULTIPLE MISSTEPS

Although cyberattacks have become ubiquitous, the response to them should be considered anything but routine. In September 2017, the consumer credit reporting agency Equifax dropped a bombshell: in a data breach between May and July of that year, hackers had access to the personal information of 143 million people.[2]

Less than 24 hours after Equifax shared the news, critics condemned the brand for seemingly going through the motions with its response: a simple, pro forma apology; free identity-theft protection and credit monitoring; and a public statement issued a month after the company discovered the breach.

It was also widely reported that three of its executives sold nearly $2 million in stock during that gap in time.[3] Additionally, social media was buzzing with the revelation that, just by registering on the site to see if their information was exposed, consumers had to agree to arbitration, waiving their right to be part of a class-action suit.[4]

For many consumers, the response perpetuated the belief that big business is just a bunch of fat cats looking out only for themselves. It didn't take long for the New York state attorney general to open an investigation. Additionally, an exclusive in the *New York Post* on September 8, 2017, suggested Equifax was shifting blame to its software provider for the data breach, thus violating another crisis commandment: be accountable.[5]

Any organization can be the target of cybercriminals. But it was Equifax's handling of the crisis that made it the target of such ridicule. That's disappointing, to say the least, for a credit company that claims to have the best interests of consumers at the heart of its business.

5. Don't Go Underground

Like the ostrich that sticks its head in the sand, the worst thing you can do is ignore the situation and hope it goes away. Whether an organization is directly responsible for an issue or not, it has an obligation to its stakeholders to manage the crisis competently.

Even if you're limited in what you can say publicly due to legal considerations or a lack of information, you can always say *something*. Refusing to accept the reality of the moment will only make you look weak and ineffective, as if you have something to hide. A communications professional should be the contact who fields requests from media and other stakeholders. Any colleagues who receive inquiries should immediately forward them to this individual, who can provide a statement or perhaps a spokesperson for an interview. This ensures the brand speaks with one voice. Such statements might include:

- "We are aware of the [situation] and are currently working to get more information."

- "We are working to learn more about the [situation] and will provide an update as soon as we are able."

- "We have been notified of the [situation] and are currently responding. As soon as we know more, we will provide an update."

Ensuring you're responsive includes checking emails and voice mails outside of 9-to-5, Monday through Friday, so if a serious issue needs addressing or a reporter is on deadline, you don't miss an opportunity to convey that you're on top of the situation.

In the introduction, I cited the case of a Massachusetts utility company that took four hours to communicate with the public during a natural gas leak. Multiple homes caught fire, and a young man lost his life. Remember that even if a brand is actively engaged in crisis *management*, a lack of effective crisis *communications*, especially when the public is at risk, will be a reputation killer every time.

6. Always Tell the Truth

Admittedly, I still cringe when someone labels what I do as "spin." That's because I equate this characterization with stretching the truth, mischaracterizing a situation, obfuscating the facts, or doing whatever necessary, perhaps even blatantly lying, to get a client out of a precarious spot.

I'm immensely proud of the work my colleagues and I are engaged in because integrity lies at the center of everything we do, in our partnership with clients and our dealings with the media. We don't lie or engage in smear campaigns, nor do we work with clients who would ask us to do so on their behalf.

There are many times when we're retained by outside legal counsel or an internal representative of an organization who acknowledge up front that a particular decision, in hindsight, wasn't the right call, and now a group of key stakeholders is angry or upset as a result. Other times, a client is accused of something they insist they didn't do, or perhaps there's a genuine difference of opinion between two parties. The issue threatens to blow up and so we're asked to help the client explain what occurred, why it happened, and how they'll make amends and move forward in a positive way.

7. Keep Your Eye on the Ball

Often, a client's instinct in responding to a crisis, especially when they believe they're in the right, is to provide *too much* information. This typically stems from a genuine desire to explain all facets of a situation to those who are looking for answers. But in crisis response, with defense often the name of the game, we usually advise direct, to-the-point language when drafting communications.

Resist the urge to include points on which you might feel vulnerable or insecure but that don't contribute to a strong message. Why volunteer information that no one is asking about or that doesn't benefit the organization? Doing so can open another front in a battle you don't need to be fighting. Instead, try to maintain a laser-like focus on the issue at hand.

There is often so much an organization wants to express, explain, or defend in a statement. This is typically informed by the long, complex history around a particular issue of which they have intimate knowledge. But frequently, you'll be drafting communications for individuals who will be hearing about the issue for the first time. So keep messages lean and free of extemporaneous language, which will ensure you don't leave any room for someone to misinterpret what you're saying. A less-is-more approach often means boiling statements, letters, and answers to questions down to their essence, to trim the excess and keep only that which drives the message forward.

There's another reason for keeping statements brief: the more you say, the less likely those with whom you're communicating will focus on the exact message you want them to. When dealing with the media, what you say or write will likely be edited for space or time unless it's a live interview. So make sure that any sentence, standing alone, is potent enough to effectively articulate your main point.

8. Don't Overcomplicate

Avoid overly complex language such as industry jargon when communicating in a crisis. A public statement needs to be obvious in its message and its meaning should be easy to understand. Overly technical explanations can sound aloof, even dismissive, to those suffering or negatively impacted by an issue or event. It also implies that your brand prioritizes process over people, which is never a good look.

The fact is that simple, clear messages can be more challenging to draft than complicated ones. As the witticism "I apologize for such a long letter—I didn't have time to write a short one" suggests, determining what language is *not* essential to a message requires a critical eye. Push back against those married to certain language or ideas that, in reality, aren't vital and necessary to communicate.

A ROBIN HOOD IN REVERSE?

In January 2021, a Reddit message board sparked an unprecedented trading frenzy of protest against the Wall Street establishment. The retail trading app Robinhood found itself at the center of one of the year's biggest PR crises after its platform shut down the trading of hot stocks GameStop and AMC Theatres.

Already facing scrutiny from regulators who were concerned that the company encouraged risky behavior, Robinhood now infuriated the very retail traders it had built its reputation on empowering. Users alleged the shutdown unfairly benefited more prominent investors. Unlike its heroic namesake from English literature, Robinhood was accused of allowing the rich to prosper even further.

CEO Vlad Tenev didn't communicate about the decision until an entire day of trading had passed. Then, when he did, he made matters significantly worse by demonstrating little empathy and spouting a hodgepodge of financial jargon. A sample of what Tenev told CNBC in a live appearance:

> We have SEC net capital requirements and clearinghouse deposits. So that's money that we have to deposit at various clearinghouses. Some of these requirements fluctuate quite a bit based on volatility in the market, and they can be substantial in the current environment where there's a lot of volatility and a lot of concentrated activity in these names that have been going viral on social media.[6]

As a result of its decision and how it communicated to its community about it, Robinhood was cast as the villain. To emphasize the magnitude of the crisis, 56 percent of its account holders considered leaving the platform in the immediate aftermath of the debacle.[7] In the wake of this widespread condemnation, Robinhood continued to deal with reputational issues even a year later.

9. Expect That Everything Will Become Public

There are too many ways to record a conversation, capture a screenshot of a social media post, or find archived web content. In addition, a proliferation in the ways we talk with one another when working remotely, including instant messaging and videoconferencing tools like Slack, Microsoft Office, and Zoom, makes it increasingly challenging to ensure that any communication remains confidential.

Every communication can easily be forwarded and shared via email or social media. When a company responds to a customer online or sends an email to its employees, it should never expect those communications to remain private, within a "circle of trust."

Before hitting Send on an email, we remind clients to ask themselves: "Will I be comfortable if this communication (intended for employees, students, board members, etc.) appears on the front page of the local newspaper?" Stopping to ask this simple question is even more critical when a crisis response is actively being followed and reported on. By adopting this mindset, chances are you won't be tempted to overshare. A little paranoia during a vulnerable time can be a good thing when thinking through all the ways your brand's reputation might come under siege.

A cover-up rarely stays under wraps, so why attempt to fabricate one in the name of hiding some ugly truths and taking the easy way out? It's *always* better to swallow a bitter pill if it ensures your organization's long-term health, viability, and continued trustworthiness. A dishonest reputation is tough to shake, but if a brand is open and honest, stakeholders almost always tend to be forgiving.

Not sharing what you know to protect image or profits has been responsible for much human trauma and suffering. Consider if, instead of being transferred between parishes, pedophile priests had been appropriately reprimanded, expelled from the priesthood, and criminally charged. Or if Big Tobacco had revealed, immediately, when they "knew and for the most part accepted the evidence that cigarette smoking was a cause of cancer by the late 1950s."[8] Yet it wasn't until 1966 that the United States became the first country in the world to require a health warning on cigarette packages.[9]

10. Anticipate What's Next

A crisis issue or event tends to be fluid, so the response strategy should remain flexible to adapt to the ever-changing reality on the ground, which might take an unexpected turn at a moment's notice. That's why it's critical to continually assess whether the current strategy is the best possible path forward. These evaluations could mean everything from monitoring office chatter and social media for unexpected new developments to identifying triggers for public attention or media coverage. Think court appearances, quarterly earnings reports, a shareholder meeting, or a planned demonstration outside company headquarters.

If you're aware of anniversary dates on which stakeholders will expect to hear from you, there's simply no excuse to be caught flat-footed. By anticipating and planning, you can avoid a second potential crisis: the impression that your organization's leadership doesn't take a situation seriously or care enough to consider the impact that certain milestones might have on victims or their loved ones.

Consider pausing planned social media content if necessary or postponing an event that might come off as tone-deaf during or in the immediate aftermath of a reputational crisis. Similarly, avoid language that may have taken on new meaning due to unfortunate timely events. For example, the Giant Food supermarket chain was heavily criticized in November 2020 when it advertised a "super spread" beside images of a wholesome and traditional Thanksgiving meal.[10] The issue? The ad was published in the throes of the COVID-19 pandemic. The term *superspreader* had taken on a whole new meaning and was commonly associated with a singular event spurring a large outbreak.

DEBRIEF

My colleagues and I are often counted on to help de-escalate a situation and ensure that our clients are portrayed in the best possible light.

Yet there's no one playbook. Each situation necessitates a customized approach. Even so, I've found there are certain assumptions that can safely be made when responding to the majority of crises. These include:

1. Plan ahead.

2. Inform and educate.

3. Be accountable.

4. Respond rapidly.

5. Don't go underground.

6. Always tell the truth.

7. Keep your eye on the ball.

8. Don't overcomplicate.

9. Expect that everything will become public.

10. Anticipate what's next.

These absolutes in responding to an issue or crisis are applicable across discipline, regardless of the sector. Understanding how and when to communicate in crisis can often be a dynamic and complicated exercise. Following these 10 commandments is the best primer possible to navigating complex, highly leveraged situations like a pro.

4

REPUTATION ROAD MAP
AUDIENCES AND CHANNELS

DURING THE DECADE I worked in local news, the audience watching our broadcasts was closely measured by the percentage of households tuned in to our newscast versus the competition's. What place stations finished in (first, second, third, etc.) during four ratings periods each year determined advertising rates and, as a result, how profitable each station was.

When I worked at the network, that data was even more insightful, providing my ABC News colleagues and me with a demographic snapshot of who was watching. This profile included categories such as gender and age group. You may have heard of the coveted viewer group "adults 18–49," which primarily sets the ad rates for entertainment programming. Over the years, most media have moved from traditional ratings points (one point equals 1.28 million people) to the metric of "impressions" to account for the multitude of platforms and times during which consumers watch on-demand programming.[1]

In pursuit of ratings (or *eyeballs* as we'd sometimes refer to them), producers often decided *what* stories would run *when* based on *who* was watching at that particular time of day (e.g., the audience tuning in to morning news programs skews heavily female). Once appointment viewing for households across the country, the traditional evening news-cast now attracts mainly older viewers like baby boomers. If you really want to know who's watching, keep track of the ads that run during that time block and consider the target audience for those products and services.

Just as a news producer might tailor a program's rundown of stories to a specific demographic, so are strategic communications targeted to those groups the messages are intended for. There are plenty of instances when we're working on issues for which the media is, in fact, one of the *least* important stakeholder groups. For example, a large company's key audiences will consist of employees, customers, the board of directors, and maybe stockholders as well as regulators and local lawmakers. In higher education, they will be students and their families, alumni, donors, board members, along with potential students.

Communicating thoughtfully in ways that enhance your reputation requires being acutely aware of what your audiences want and need to hear at times of uncertainty. For instance, how do you persuade prospective patients to seek treatment at your hospital if it's gaining notoriety for a tragic mistake during a procedure or a surgery? How do you persuade a parent to send their child to a university that recently made headlines due to one of its faculty members being accused of sexual misconduct?

TALKING TO YOUR AUDIENCES

Here are questions to ask yourself, the answers to which will help inform the best way to communicate with those most important to you.

Who Should Be Told First?

When deciding who needs to hear important news first, it's best to think about the order from the inside out. Your internal community such as employees, staff, board members, students, or faculty are your biggest boosters. They have the most skin in the game, care about the company more than anyone else, and are potential ambassadors for your brand. As a result, they should always hear about new developments directly from leadership first, not from the media or another source.

Armed with the proper messaging, these internal stakeholders can be your most effective emissaries, helping to shore up the defense of your brand. The strategy known as *cascading communications* refers to sharing the information with management first and having them deliver the message to their direct reports and so on down through the entire organization.

Is the Messaging Consistent?

While communications should be customized for individual stakeholder groups, the core messaging and rationale behind the leadership's key decisions should remain consistent. That way, everyone will be "singing from the same song sheet," as the expression goes. Conversely, messaging that varies from audience to audience can result in a great deal of confusion, uncertainty, and numerous follow-up questions.

If it's revealed that customers and vendors are receiving different answers to the same questions, you'll appear to be less than honest and forthcoming. Avoid telling each audience what it wants to hear because it might be seen like the easy way out at the time. Keep in mind there's a record of every written communication. If you think you can get away with an inconsistency by, say, deleting a social media post, you can bet someone has already captured a screenshot of it and will call you out for your hypocrisy. Don't take that chance.

Who Is Being Talked To?

We typically divide audiences between those on the inside such as employees and board members and those on the outside such as the public and the press. The answers to the questions "How familiar are they with your brand?" and "How invested are they in your success?" should influence the tone of communications, how much context you need to provide, and most importantly, what information you share.

Stakeholders come from a variety of places, both literal and figurative. They possess various levels of knowledge and opinions about a brand. Most importantly, they care about different things and might want individual concerns addressed.

None of us is a blank canvas; we all arrive at an issue or event with a certain perspective, including some preconceived notions and bias. Tailoring messaging for distinct audiences will help ensure that brands meet each individual audience member *where they are*. Additionally, it ensures that messaging doesn't come across as tone-deaf.

For example, citing last quarter's profit margin makes sense for an investor but not for a customer whose personal information was exposed when your business was the target of a data breach. Ask yourself what's top of mind for a target group and address those issues head-on. It'll allow you to get out in front of a potential crisis or, at the very least, prevent one from escalating.

Who Is Being Talked Through?

Let's say you're doing an interview with a local radio program. In reality, you're talking to their listeners *through* the show's host(s) asking the questions. Aside from preparing for the subject matter, game-plan for what questions will likely be asked based on the hosts, the types of questions they typically ask, past stories or interviews, and the outlet they work for. Suppose it's a general news outlet like a daily newspaper or local television network affiliate. You can typically expect questions to be more consumer-focused and less of a deep dive into the nitty-gritty of a particular sector or industry. If it's a trade or business publication, questions will be asked to elicit a more high-level response for the readership who will likely possess some depth of knowledge around the topic.

When prepping clients ahead of a media opportunity, we provide them with the background and tendencies of the reporter they'll be speaking with. For instance, some journalists ask a lot of follow-up questions, while others tend to interrupt often. Arming our clients with this kind of intel beforehand helps them calibrate their answers accordingly.

On live broadcast appearances, producers will often line up more than one guest at a time, and so a client may be sharing screen time with another individual, perhaps even a competitor. How does that guest typically conduct themselves in an interview? Can other guests get a word in, or do they tend to hoard the airtime?

How Are Stakeholders Used to Hearing News?

Where someone is can refer to their state of mind, belief system, or, in a more literal sense, the social or traditional media channel where they regularly get their news and information.

When determining the channel on which to communicate, consider the urgency of the situation. For instance, if it's a relatively minor issue, don't send a text message which may alarm recipients because they're only used to receiving the most important and time-sensitive messages that way. Also weigh the skillset of your organization's top executives. If your CEO is known more for their savvy business sense than for being a great communicator, think about a well-crafted email. However, if the crisis requires an in-person gathering, consider splitting up leadership responsibilities, such as having the CEO make opening remarks while top lieutenants field questions from those gathered.

CHOOSING YOUR CHANNEL

Discerning *which* channel(s) to disseminate information over is one of the first things we settle on with our clients. With the proliferation of digital solutions and platforms, more choices are available to communicators than ever. Yet *how* your audience receives messages in times of crisis can help shape the perception of how up-front or less than forthright a brand is willing to be.

Website

A question we get asked often is, "Should we post language in response to a crisis on our website?" We typically recommend a banner on the homepage that users can click to see a statement if they're interested. Some clients choose to archive or "warehouse" all communications on their website, so they're readily accessible at all times.

One benefit of having your crisis statement housed on your site is that you can easily share the URL on social media channels. For example, "To read a message from our CEO on [insert crisis], please click here" is often more practical than posting the entire statement. This approach can be beneficial on a channel like Twitter, which limits word count (280 characters as of this writing).

For instance, Atlassian, an Australian software company, posted a short statement on Twitter in the spring of 2020 expressing its support for the Black Lives Matter movement. In the same tweet, the brand linked to a more full-throated letter from the company's CEO and founder. He spoke about his fervent belief in equality and human rights and stated, "Atlassian cares deeply about supporting our team, our communities, our planet and our customers."[2]

A second example was in 2021, when Furniture Village, Britain's largest independent furniture retailer, posted a short statement on Twitter in response to a cyberattack. The brand apologized for having to shut down its phone lines, assuring customers that their data was secure and that the company was working as quickly as it could to get up and running again. In the same tweet, the company linked to updates and dated statements on its website along with FAQs for concerned customers.[3]

Email

Still the most effective and efficient way to blast out a timely message to a large group, email is more formal than social media and can be easily referenced at a later date or forwarded to those not on the original distribution list.

Don't overwhelm recipients with information. Identify the problem, what the expected impact will be, and what is being done to mitigate the issue. Take the time to thoughtfully consider every sentence and how it could be interpreted and potentially twisted by skeptics or adversaries. Make sure there's consensus on the final draft and have an attorney vet the language if necessary.

The mechanics of sending an email are just as important, such as ensuring that the message is formatted properly and readable regardless of the device. Similar to how you would review a marketing email, confirm the open rates and the percentage of recipients who click through to any hyperlinks to provide a clearer picture of how the message was received. If the rates are determined to be insufficient, consider a follow-up communication.

THE PESO MODEL

Marketers today often refer to the PESO model of an effective and integrated communications strategy.[4] If you want to ensure your message reaches a broad audience, you'll need to consider some combination of these four channels:

Paid. This refers to traditional or online advertising. These opportunities include "sponsored content" in traditional media outlets, with the search for additional revenue streams having blurred the lines between business and editorial.

Earned. This is traditional media relations. Placement of a story in a third-party media outlet based on merit, i.e., the perceived news value (public interest) of the story.

Shared. This refers to social media, the most immediate and cost-effective way of widely disseminating information beyond your own community. It cuts out any traditional media middleman who would edit or potentially water down your message.

Owned. This is any property owned and controlled by your brand, such as a website or blog. What sets this channel apart from Shared is that the public can engage with social media and validate or reject messages in real time.

Each channel is more powerful when leveraged along with another. For instance, if media relations professionals secure a newspaper story and then share it on Facebook with a paid or boosted post, that is a combination of Earned, Shared, and Paid. If a blog post on the company's website is then shared on its LinkedIn platform with a boosted post, that is a combination of Owned, Shared, and Paid.

Social Media

Posting a full statement on social media offers both benefits and drawbacks. One of the advantages is it allows the whole world to reference your response in one location. Plus, you don't need to send it to the media or other stakeholders separately; they can merely pull quotes from your page or feed.

The downside is that both good and bad feedback can be posted publicly below a statement. We advise clients against turning off the comments below such messaging because users may interpret this as an effort to stifle free speech. I'll talk more about how to manage social media to safeguard your reputation in chapter 9.

Each digital platform tends to attract a particular type of user. If you're focused on a business audience, LinkedIn is your best bet. Communicating with parents? Try Facebook. If you're trying to reach those between sixteen and twenty-four years old, you'll find them on TikTok. If you want to connect with thought leaders like journalists or politicians, start a conversation on Twitter.

Be sure to customize your message not only for the audience, but also for the channel's culture. That means employing the appropriate word count, hashtags, and links suitable for each platform.

Video

Video is a valuable tool both when there's time for brainstorming and extensive pre-production, and when communicating during a fast-moving crisis. A spokesperson speaking on camera communicates a high degree of transparency, even if they're unable to share every detail.

It demonstrates a willingness to put a face on your brand, even at a difficult time.

Ensure the script strikes the appropriate tone and that it's been carefully vetted by communications and legal counsel. Prep ahead of time so your spokesperson is familiar with the writing and can deliver the words as if it's second nature and not as if they're reading them for the first time. If the script is lengthy, consider filming with a teleprompter. This will take some practice so it feels natural and doesn't appear as if your spokesperson is merely reading words on a screen.

Recording and editing video can take relatively little time. Like a breaking news story, clips can be turned around fast (sometimes in under an hour) in the hands of professionals. Video is also the one medium that can be most effectively shared across earned media. TV outlets will use clips from the video, radio will pull the audio, and print outlets can use quotes.

Town Hall Meetings

Often geared toward internal stakeholders such as employees, town hall meetings can be effective forums for addressing a number of different issues and, if necessary, clearing the air. They encourage open dialogue and accountability, providing those in the audience with a forum to voice their opinions and ask questions.

To keep the town hall organized and on track, have a clear opening message. Stating the goals of the get-together at the outset will help ensure everyone leaves feeling like they're on the same page. Some town halls can get derailed if there's the perception that concerns expressed are being belittled, or if one of the speakers is dodging a question. If there's enough time, try a dry run ahead of time and practice answering the tough questions.

The larger the audience, the more managers should be on hand to answer questions. I've witnessed town halls where those with similar concerns or complaints joined forces and ganged up on the manager answering questions at the time. At the very least, additional personnel should be available to come to their colleague's defense if need be to provide additional context or perspectives. Especially in large companies, where employees don't get much face time with upper management, town halls provide significant opportunities to strengthen workplace culture and boost morale.

LEVERAGING VIDEO IN A CRISIS

Mary Barra had only been on the job as CEO of General Motors for a couple of months when she appeared in an internal video to address the recalls of more than three million cars to which hundreds of deaths had been linked.[5] She admitted the company was at fault in stark terms: "Something went wrong with our process in this instance, and terrible things happened."[6]

Speaking as a CEO and "as a mom with a family of my own," Barra reiterated the company's apology and committed to fixing any lingering and systemic issues with how GM handled recalls. She provided a list of action items, including the creation of a "global vehicle safety role," additional staffing at call centers to handle customer questions, and mailing of recall letters to affected owners.[7]

Barra's tone, body language, and facial expression communicated regret, sincerity, and competency, in a way that a written statement could not. The new CEO looked directly into the camera without flinching, communicating clearly that the buck stopped with her.

Realizing that taking out full-page ads in newspapers across the country alone wouldn't suffice, GM produced the internal video, which they knew would be shared externally and picked up by media. In essence, GM was collaborating on the coverage of a crisis that was already in the headlines.

Departmental Meetings

The smaller the group, the easier the dynamic is to navigate. Colleagues in the same department have likely collaborated in the past, making them more apt to understand one another's thought processes. Therefore, less will be lost in translation and questions can be more easily anticipated by the manager leading the meeting.

A more intimate setting also allows managers to effectively address how a crisis will impact a specific department or group. Will employee roles change? Are there new protocols in place? Will the reporting structure remain the same? Gathered with familiar colleagues, participants will feel less intimidated to speak up and offer candid feedback, the substance of which can help identify vulnerabilities that leadership hadn't considered.

One-on-One Meetings

This intimate setting is particularly helpful when sensitive or confidential information will be discussed. It provides uninterrupted time with an individual who may be uniquely impacted by an issue or event and ensures they receive the resources or support they require. It lessens the likelihood of follow-up questions or something said being lost in translation.

One-on-ones also act as a practical listening tool to understand an individual team member's most significant concerns. Patterns could emerge to help identify unanticipated or unplanned-for issues and vulnerabilities. The personal nature of the meeting can build trust at a critical time for an organization.

Texting

By now, we're all used to receiving text messages and other notifications on our phones such as when there's an AMBER Alert or severe and threatening weather in the immediate area. Texts, officially known as SMS (short message service) messages, are effective in communicating time-sensitive and urgent information because it's virtually guaranteed that everyone sent one will see it.

SMS as a channel has been especially useful in public health emergencies.

- The Red Cross successfully uses text messaging to activate its community of blood donors. Information shared includes donation locations and urgent appeals for donations to people with rare blood types.

- The National Health Service, the publicly funded healthcare system in England, launched a text message support service in 2020 for people with COVID-19. The messages asked patients about their well-being and provided support to those who needed it during their isolation period.[8]

Employers can be assured their team members will be carrying their phones with them most of the time whether they're at their desks, on the go, or if it's before, during, or after work. This is why texting is the best way to reach the entire organization during a crisis that presents a clear and present danger, such as an active shooter, a fire, or demonstrations blocking access to a building. As with media statements, having template language ready to go and a clear approval process is the best way to prepare for such a necessity.

According to the global research and advisory firm Gartner, open rates are as high as 98 percent for SMS, compared with just 20 percent for email.[9] The downside is that some users will feel as though you're infringing upon their private space, so make sure they can opt in or out of future text messages.

DEBRIEF

It's easier to persuade another to see your side if you start, not from where you are, but where *they* are. When deciding how communications should be positioned and how they should be disseminated, ask yourself the questions offered in this chapter:

- Who should be told first?

- Is the messaging consistent?

- Who is being talked to?

- Who is being talked through?

- How are stakeholders used to hearing news?

When strategizing, rely on crisis team members (you can read more about crisis teams in chapter 5) who regularly engage with your target audience. They'll know what these groups are likely to be most concerned about after hearing important or troubling news and what they need so they don't lose trust and confidence in your organization.

How stakeholders receive important, complex, or difficult news should be determined by the organization's culture and by recent history. How are they used to hearing from you? Will a text message feel in tune with past communications, or will it signal such urgency that stakeholders might feel those in charge have lost control? Ask yourself which of the following channels is right for the moment:

- website

- email

- social media

- video

- town hall meetings

- departmental meetings

- one-on-one meetings

- texting

The number of communications options that today's consumers have at their fingertips and where they spend their time on- and offline is practically infinite. So, whether your strategy goes by PESO or another name, find an integrated solution that ensures your messages reach everyone with whom you need to remain in touch.

5

A PLAN TO PROTECT
AND DEFEND

CONSIDER THE STUDY I referenced in chapter 3, in which just 62 percent of respondents said they were familiar with their company's crisis plan. The study also revealed that approximately 13 percent of respondents knew that a plan existed but had never seen it, more than 10 percent weren't sure if one existed, and more than 13 percent said they had no crisis plan at all.[1] A failure to plan for the inevitable isn't just head scratching; it's a dereliction of duty on the part of any organization, regardless of size.

An updated and comprehensive written plan is *the* crucial piece in anticipating, navigating, and mitigating the risks that threaten your reputation. Just having that plan, however, isn't enough if it's tucked away in an obscure file. It should be a living document, updated as often as necessary, such as when members of the crisis response team leave the company or come aboard, when policies change, and when new vulnerabilities are identified.

The responsibility of maintaining and updating the plan should belong to the communications lead or chief of staff, depending on how an organization is structured.

The document should be as action-oriented and intuitive as possible. This means prioritizing those elements likely to be most frequently used. Response procedures for rare scenarios should be included in an appendix. There's no reason to have them up-front alongside reputational threats most likely to occur.

Plans will vary depending on the organization and the number of potential scenarios that would qualify as a true reputational "crisis." Regardless of the brand, however, all plans should start with the following activities.

CHOOSING A CRISIS RESPONSE TEAM

There should be a core group of managers responsible for the crisis response. Because there's no way to predict the nature of future crises, it should be an interdisciplinary team that includes members of the C-suite as well as legal and communications counsel.

Other members should be determined by what business function is impacted by the crisis; those department heads and managers will possess the subject matter expertise to understand the implications of what occurred and the potential fallout as well as possible strategies to diminish the threat. Examples include the head of information technology (IT) during a data breach or the director of human resources (HR) when dealing with an employee-specific issue. Although each team member should have a clear understanding of their division's or department's role in a particular crisis, keep in mind that any situation that rises to *true* emergency levels will impact an entire organization.

In the event of a serious cyberattack or an alleged financial crime, outside counsel (e.g., legal, communications, and forensic) should lead the investigation rather than in-house managers who may be motivated by a strong desire to avoid blame. In those moments, it's critical to maintain objectivity in collecting evidence. Outside counsel will possess the expertise and experience to guide an organization through industry, state, or federal reporting requirements. In addition, having an attorney on board maintains privilege over communications in which they're included, providing greater protection from what information may or may not be admissible in potential litigation.

Anyone whose responsibilities include crisis management knows these events aren't confined to regular business hours. That's why redundancy in assigned personnel is critical in forming an agile group capable of responding 24/7/365. Each crisis team member should have a designated backup who can carry out that role's function and responsibilities if that member is ill, on vacation, out of the country, or otherwise unavailable.

Although you might think it goes without saying, crisis team members should be familiar enough with one another to collaborate effectively in a stressful situation. There have actually been occasions when a client retained our services in the midst of a full-blown crisis, only for us to learn that some of their internal crisis team members didn't know one other. Yet, when time was of the essence, they were expected to operate like a well-oiled machine. Not ideal, to say the least.

The more time spent together preparing for the real thing, the more opportunities to build camaraderie. Exercises like tabletop drills (discussed in chapter 7) are especially helpful in familiarizing team members with how everyone makes decisions when navigating the rigors of an actual crisis.

How decisions are made will also depend on the CEO's leadership style. Do they like to go around the table and hear from everyone? Do they call on certain individuals in the room or on the call? Or is it more of a free-for-all, with participants endorsing or taking issue with a particular perspective or recommendation? Most of the time, multiple participants offer input or answer questions from the CEO who, as the ultimate decision maker, will choose to take or leave that counsel.

ESTABLISHING RESPONSE PROTOCOLS

At the heart of any crisis plan are the prescribed steps to take in response to an event or issue deemed a crisis. Each team member has a role to play.

For large organizations that could face a greater number of possible threats, we tier sets of crisis procedures. Each assigned tier is based on several factors, including the time sensitivity of the event/issue and the likelihood of the crisis attracting outside attention, including media coverage. Tier 1 is usually reserved for more urgent matters, while tier 2 is for those that are less severe. Sometimes, there is even a tier 3 for crises that are slow moving, affording the organization extra time to respond.

SAMPLE RESPONSE PROTOCOLS

For example, the first action steps for a tier 1 crisis confronted by a school transportation company might be as follows:

1. If the incident requires notifying first responders or law enforcement, the dispatcher or operations manager will contact the appropriate agency to respond to the emergency. If immediate notification of first responders or law enforcement is not required, the dispatcher or operations manager will proceed to the next steps.

2. The dispatcher who learns of the matter first will report the incident to the operations manager, who will contact a vice president, who will then notify the president. The president will contact the school district.

3. Notification of families should be coordinated with the school district. If the company is unable to reach any key school district personnel, then and only then should the company contact the families of students involved in the incident without speaking to the district first.

4. A meeting or conference call should be set up as soon as possible with the crisis response team, which will determine what type of additional communication for different stakeholders is necessary.

Tier 2 protocols for the same company might look something like this:

1. If the incident occurs during work hours, the dispatcher contacts the operations manager, who will contact the vice president, who will then notify the president.

2. If the incident arises after business hours or on the weekend, the employee who is notified first should contact an operations manager, who should then contact a vice president, who should then contact the president.

3. The president will use his discretion to determine the timing of a call with the crisis team that consists of all or some of its members.

4. This crisis team will determine whether communication to any audience is necessary and, if so, whether contact should occur by email or phone.

Readily apparent is the greater sense of urgency in the first set of protocols. This is because of the logistics, coordination, and notification necessary in a time-sensitive crisis like a vehicle accident. In contrast, the second set of protocols is more flexible in that the timing can be determined by those in charge of the response.

Depending on the size of your crisis team and the number of outside partners you may need to notify or consult, consider a communications flow chart to illustrate how notification should occur and how information should travel from one team member to another. Exhibit 1 is a sample flow chart for a construction company.

This visual hierarchy illustrates the flow of information from one manager to another, setting the company up for an efficient and effective response. The purpose is to avoid wasted time and to prioritize sharing information with those who can directly impact the outcome of the crisis based on their job function, their own contacts, and the decisions they have the authority to sign off on.

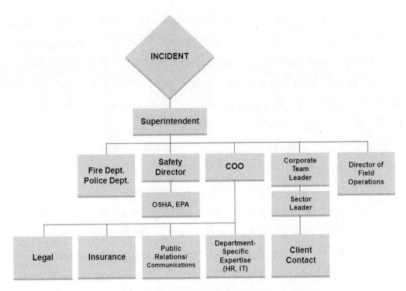

EXHIBIT 1 COMMUNICATIONS FLOW CHART

Part of the assigned responsibilities under Public Relations/Communications should include social media monitoring, which I'll discuss further in chapter 9. Online activity can be an important barometer of the public's response and concern in a crisis. Seeing these conversations in real time allows a brand to calibrate its response or to pivot, if necessary, to messages that are more successfully resonating with stakeholder groups.

ENGAGING WITH THE MEDIA

Have clear directions for staff if reporters call, email, or unexpectedly show up at the office. Anyone who could be the first point of contact, including a receptionist or security official, should be familiar with these procedures.

If you're anticipating media outreach, it's a good idea to remind employees, board members, and anyone else who could be approached that they're *not* designated to speak on behalf of the organization. Even well-intentioned individuals can end up saying the wrong thing and be misquoted by the press as "a company spokesperson."

Instruct those staff to provide the name and phone number of a media contact at the company who can help facilitate a response. Another option is for the employee to take down the reporter's contact information and to let them know someone will get back to them shortly. This route allows communications professionals to be quickly looped in so they can respond and vet the opportunity in a timely manner. Collectively, the crisis team can then determine what type of response, if any, they want to offer.

Advice for those whom a reporter confronts: never utter the words *no comment*, never physically place your hands on a reporter or a camera, and never cover your face. Although there might be an instinct to react in such a way, the optics of such aggressive actions communicate, if not guilt, a wish to hide something. However, because your office is private property, you have every right to politely ask a reporter and photographer to stop filming.

In certain matters, clients have reached out to report that "one of our employees received an email from a reporter who wants to speak with them, and they want to know how to respond." Because the appearance of muzzling employees can negatively impact a brand's image, we suggest telling the individual that they're free to do as they like—but that they're under no obligation to speak with the reporter. Doing this avoids the appearance of management coming across as heavy handed, as if it's trying to silence or censor employees.

Those who aren't used to engaging with the media often believe that if they're called by a reporter or have a microphone shoved in their face, they're *obligated* to speak with them. Not expecting such an encounter, some people freeze or, out of a sense of politeness, forget that they are free *not* to speak. As most individuals have no direct or regular contact with the media, it's not surprising they're unclear on the rules of engagement.

DRAFTING TEMPLATE STATEMENTS

Essential to responding to media and other inquiries in a timely fashion is having ready-to-go language that doesn't have to be drafted from scratch in the middle of a crisis when every team member is under additional pressure. Therefore, we typically include at least a dozen template statements to help clients understand, anticipate, and plan for the broad range of potential issues their organization could face.

Crises that we have created template language for include but are not limited to:

bomb threats	hostage situations	pandemics
lawsuits	offensive social media posts	injuries/fatalities
data breaches	executive misconduct	industrial accidents
terrorist attacks	fires	active shooter
sexual misconduct	evacuations	natural disasters

As I recommended in the crisis commandment, "Keep your Eye on the Ball," keep messages brief and to the point. That way, if an outlet does use only a sentence or two, they're potent enough to communicate the most vital information. Resist the urge to overdo it and include more than necessary.

Public statements during a crisis are also opportunities to reinforce your organization's values and mission.

For example, if a former employee accuses a manager of making racially insensitive remarks, the statement in response to inquiries should include that organization's values around diversity and tolerance:

An inclusive office environment is key to our firm's culture and success and we do not tolerate any form of harassment, intimidation, or bullying. Any employees found to have participated in such behavior will be disciplined up to and including termination.

In another example, a worker is injured on a job site or at a manufacturing facility. After stating what occurred, the company should stress the importance of safety as part of its day-to-day operations:

> *The health and well-being of all our employees and subcontractors is our top priority.*

This language can easily be adapted for additional external or internal communications. So, if the need to share information immediately is through a community-wide letter, for instance, you have the building blocks ready to go when time is of the essence.

CRISIS PLANNING FOR SMALL ORGANIZATIONS

Not every company has a communications department or even a designated staff member in charge of marketing or public relations. Although most principles of crisis communications and issues management are consistent across sectors, small businesses and nonprofits might need to prioritize some aspects of planning over others due to limited resources.

Yet, regardless of size, any organization can plan for how it will respond to those crises they're most likely to confront. The Small Business Administration (SBA), the Federal Emergency Management Agency (FEMA), and even the Internal Revenue Service (IRS) have free resources available on their websites that cover everything from crisis planning and training to applying for financial assistance after a disaster.[2]

All organizations, big and small, should have a contact list for key staff or outside resources (e.g., an attorney, a PR rep). In addition, a one-page outline of clear response steps in the event of an emergency is the bare minimum each company needs to have on hand. After all, the smaller the organization, presumably the shorter the list of likely crisis scenarios to anticipate.

ASSEMBLING WRITTEN TOOLS

My role as a counselor of crisis communications consists, for the most part, of three main functions:

1. Offering counsel and strategy recommendations

2. Drafting language our clients use in various situations, some intended to be delivered on paper, others to be spoken in person

3. Engaging with reporters on our clients' behalf to ensure their interests are represented

At times, the planning can get pretty granular to ensure we've anticipated every potential scenario. For example, we've scripted voice mail messages for our clients to leave if individuals they need to reach in a timely fashion don't answer their call. We've drafted language for a receptionist who picks up the phone and hears a reporter or angry client on the other end of the line. We consider every word and ask ourselves how that term or phrase may be misinterpreted and potentially used against our client.

As discussed in the previous chapter, who you're communicating with should determine the content and tone of the language you draft. Each audience may have different questions or concerns based on how they engage with your brand. We'll often draft multiple versions of questions and answers, tailoring each for a specific audience.

For example, the primary audiences for a nonprofit organization will include:

Staff	Board	Committees
Community members	Donors	Volunteers
Partner agencies	Press	Clients

Identifying key audiences up front will allow those drafting communications to anticipate what questions each will have and what relevant information needs to be conveyed.

The C-suite culture dictates the nature of the engagement with outside communications counsel. More often than not, my colleagues and I are asked to write the first draft of a community letter or meeting script. We've also worked with plenty of CEOs, heads of schools, presidents, and executive directors who prefer to take the initial draft to ensure what's written captures their voice. Either method is acceptable.

Once the first draft is complete, feedback should be solicited from a tight circle of advisers. If you can, capture everyone's input within the same shared document so that each colleague's suggested edits and comments are visible. Doing this can help cut down on conflicting and confusing feedback.

The following are materials intended to be shared in written form.

The Overall Strategy

A memo drafted for the C-suite's review should articulate the reasoning behind the timing, sequencing, and content of all crisis communications. Provide any necessary context, such as the mindset of key stakeholder groups and the likely outcome of media coverage based on the outlet or reporter's history of similar stories.

This is also where, if there are disagreements with prior suggestions that have been made, you should feel empowered to push back with an informed opinion. Communications professionals are relied on for constructive feedback, and this is where they should offer a justification for their position. To avoid snap judgments, leaders need to understand this thinking and point of view before reviewing the draft messaging.

Part of our strategic recommendations for a client that was dealing with a significant negative issue included:

The ultimate goal of the PR strategy is to limit the coverage to one or two days. We advise against any approach that could prolong the coverage and keep the story in the headlines longer than necessary. For messaging, we recommend a contrite tone.

We will gauge the possibility of off-the-record or on-background conversations with reporters that would allow us to provide proper context around the history of the issue at hand. Information shared would not be part of the formal messaging as raising these points on the record would give the impression that the company is making excuses and refusing to accept responsibility.

Timeline

The sequencing of communications, who you tell first, second, and so forth, can make the difference between a well-received message and one that exacerbates a situation. Regardless of how well written the messaging is, an entire strategy can be sunk if it doesn't consider the parties involved and with whom they could share the news. When sensitive information is bound to spread quickly, we often recommend sharing with each group in as tight a window as possible, so everyone hears from leadership first and not from one another through a game of telephone.

As an example, a few years ago, we were handling communications for a large organization that was planning a merger with a competitor. The client was a global brand with offices on multiple continents. Precise planning was necessary to ensure that emails and meetings were sequenced in such a way so there were as few gaps as possible in announcing the big news.

A communications timeline can be as simple and straightforward as the following:

Now–mid-November	Draft and revise communications
	Coordinate sequencing and mechanics of sending emails
	Identify VIPs who should be called personally by CEO

Night before announcement	Evening video call with full board and leadership team separately
	All-staff video call invite sent for next morning
TBD	Announcement
TBD (early morning)	All-staff video call
9 a.m.	All-staff communication is sent

More complex issues and events are better organized in a planning matrix (see exhibit 2 on the next page as an example) that will account for those materials and meetings necessary to ensure the strategy can be executed on a tight timeline.

Planning for the possibility that the event might leak before launch day, we drafted short statements to provide to stakeholders if they inquired about a possible merger.

For unconfirmed rumors, the suggested response was:

It is our policy not to discuss internal business matters that may or may not be under consideration.

For confirmed information, the suggested response was:

We're not at liberty at this time to discuss any business matters that [the company] may be engaged in. We are always evaluating opportunities to ensure a successful future in which we can better serve our customers.

	PHASE 1	PHASE 2	PHASE 3/LAUNCH
COMMUNICATIONS	1. Identify spokespeople 2. Finalize cities for post-announcement events 3. Write talking points for first-line responders 4. Develop new website 5. Develop social media plan	1. Get approval for final communications schedule and stakeholder audiences 2. Draft and finalize launch press release 3. Draft email messages 4. Draft talking points for customer relations 5. Review website 6. Finalize social media plan 7. Send embargoed press release to media	1. Exclusive articles are published 2. Send merger announcement to all constituents 3. Hold town halls in New York and London 4. Set up video calls 5. Pitch news to targeted media 6. Follow up with targeted media as needed
IN-PERSON MEETINGS	1. Maintain ongoing conversations 2. Maintain ongoing planning	1. Set up video shoot for CEO 2. Train spokespeople for interviews 3. Set up media interviews	1. Make sure spokespeople are available at town hall locations 2. Hold 1:1 briefings with local public officials and community leaders 3. Reach out to business partners
ASSETS	1. Draft Q&As, talking points, and fact sheets 2. Finalize media statements 3. Create architecture and outline for new website	1. Design visuals for lobby 2. Finalize stakeholder communications 3. Create introductory video 4. Beta test new website	1. Send launch news and video to various channels 2. Push website live

EXHIBIT 2   PLANNING MATRIX

INCIDENT	ACTION STEPS	COMMUNICATIONS
Employee or visitor tests positive for COVID	1. Contact local public authorities and follow their guidance 2. Determine affected areas, path of travel, facilities used, etc. 3. Confirm individual is not on the property 4. Meet with janitorial staff to review scope of work using CDC guidance 5. Circulate draft communication 6. Monitor media	Issue office-wide communication
a. Employee lives with a person who has tested positive for COVID b. Employee has returned from a restricted area c. Employee has a suspected but unconfirmed case of COVID	1. Determine areas affected. 2. Confirm the employee is not on the property 3. Coordinate scope of work with janitorial staff 4. Circulate draft communication 5. Monitor media (For unconfirmed cases, defer steps 4 and 5 until a positive test is validated)	None needed
Employee's child has had contact with someone who has tested positive	1. Determine affected areas 2. Confirm the employee is not on the property 3. Meet with janitorial staff to review scope of work 4. Monitor media (If the employee subsequently tests positive, follow the steps in the first incident type)	None needed

EXHIBIT 3   SITUATIONAL MATRIX

If-Then Scenarios

Like a project schedule, a matrix to accommodate "if-then" scenarios features several likely crises and the corresponding actions and communications for each instance. This type of matrix allows an organization to plan for potential issues or to work through those in progress where the outcome is yet to be determined. Examples include the early stages of a pandemic, executive misconduct resulting in possible criminal charges, and product recalls.

In early 2020, before working from home became the norm in many companies, employers grappled with what to do if an employee wasn't feeling well or demonstrated symptoms of COVID-19. Questions included: "What if an employee recently traveled overseas?" and "What if an employee's child was exposed to someone with COVID?" Were those scenarios alone enough to order everyone in the office to self-quarantine?

To help clients, we created a situational matrix like exhibit 3. Each possible scenario was listed on the left, followed by the necessary action steps and the communication program rolled out on the right.

Community Letters

Set the record straight with your internal audiences before they hear about negative or otherwise significant news from another source. This group will comprise a brand's biggest supporters, so the tone should naturally be more personal than it would be for a media or public statement.

Provide any necessary context but don't bury the new information too far down. Be sure to explain how the latest developments came about, how they're being addressed, and what the path forward is. Again, never put anything in the letter that you're concerned might become public.

Here's an example of an employee letter we drafted for a business acquiring a smaller but nonetheless significant competitor:

Dear Team:

We are excited to announce that [the company being acquired] will be joining the [the acquiring company] effective today. This news will be shared with our customers and the broader market later today, but we wanted to make sure you heard it first directly from us.

This is a significant move for us and will further reinforce our leadership position in the industry. For those not familiar with [the company being acquired], it has built an outstanding reputation for its innovation, capabilities, and service excellence. The company's strengths and values align with our own. In many areas, we anticipate working closely to build deep customer relationships, to improve our supply chain, and ultimately to strengthen both companies.

Attached is the internal FAQ for reference. For those in contact with our customers, this should help address any questions you may receive.

Again, we are thrilled to share this news with you and will provide further updates in the coming weeks.
Sincerely,
[CEO]

Media Statements

Statements crafted from the template language I've described, and often referred to as "holding statements," aren't meant to be proactively distributed. Instead, they're to be used in response to inquiries.

Here's an example in the case of a company under investigation for hiring undocumented workers:

[Company name] has gone to great lengths to ensure the legality of everyone working in our warehouses with regard to their immigration status and their ability to work as an independent contractor. As we cooperate with officials during their investigation, we will continue to do everything in our power to ensure our compliance with the law.

Due to strict privacy laws, any statement on a high-profile termination should be approved only after careful consideration and legal review. Here's an example of a holding statement we drafted for a client. It balances PR considerations with the legal strategy:

[Company's name] recently learned of conduct by one of our [employees/managers] believed to be a violation of the company's standards and protocols. After a thorough internal investigation, that individual is no longer employed by the company. [The company's] leadership works every day to foster a workplace of honesty, integrity, and personal accountability. At this time, this remains a confidential employee matter.

Depending on the significance and scope of a crisis, a spokesperson may need to deliver the statement verbally before gathered media. Speaking at a formal press conference or before a gaggle of assembled journalists can be an efficient way to share information, especially if the crisis occurs at a single location. Still, this can be a risky proposition if the speaker is not fully informed or media trained, which we will discuss in detail in the next chapter.

In some situations, organizations will need to go on offense and push out a public statement. Targets may include local, regional, national, and trade outlets specific to the brand's industry. Beforehand, identity the appropriate reporters or editors to contact. If possible, select journalists you've had productive working relationships with and who cover the relevant beat.

Information will need to be shared proactively when an organization has an obligation, fiduciary or ethical (or both), to communicate with stakeholders. Such scenarios might include the chief financial officer being arrested for embezzling funds, a teacher arrested for possessing child pornography, or two parochial schools planning to merge due to decreased enrollment.

No matter how airtight your communications, there will inevitably be those who will have additional questions, comments, or concerns. Be prepared with follow-up language, such as a simple acknowledgment of receipt and appreciation. When a more in-depth response is required, reference the questions and answers that have been prepared ahead of time and which I'll address in the next section.

COMMUNICATIONS TO BE SPOKEN

Keep in mind that, even with the most well-thought-out written statements, some stakeholders will feel better if they hear news and can ask questions face-to-face. Seeing a speaker's facial expression and body language, and hearing reassurance in their voice, can go a long way in easing concerns or fears. The ability to ask questions can be the catharsis an individual needs at a time of uncertainty.

These in-person interactions are most helpful in high-stakes situations in which the entire organization will be impacted. This might be the announcement of new leadership, a merger or acquisition, a large number of layoffs, or another significant change in how a business operates or functions.

To verbally address a reputational threat, ensure you have the following messaging on hand.

Talking Points

This is the most important information you want your stakeholders to know. Talking points, or "key messages" as they are sometimes referred to, are the building blocks of communications in which a defense, justification, or argument is articulated in the appropriate and approved language. They can serve as the outline for short or more lengthy communications such as a media statement or a community letter.

Talking points should contain the timeliest and most relevant information listed in order of importance. Additionally, they should include proof points to back up your argument, whether that proof is hard (data, other quantitative metrics) or soft (stories, anecdotes). While the talking points themselves should remain high level, consider submessages to address specific issues for different audiences.

Format your talking points in bullets and keep them brief and to the point. These messages are intended to be memorized by spokespeople, so avoid too much detail as well as long explanations. I strive to keep each talking point to no more than two sentences. For the tougher subjects you would prefer not to raise for discussion, leave explanations for the Q&A, which I'll delve into next.

For instance, in a scenario in which the CFO has embezzled from his company, the talking points might include:

- We retained a respected forensic accounting firm once financial irregularities were discovered last month.

- When the firm completed its audit, we confronted [the CFO], who confessed that he had embezzled funds over the past year.

- He was terminated immediately, and we have referred the matter to the district attorney's office.

- We have completely restructured the company's financial reporting and monitoring procedures to ensure this never happens again.

Q&A

This is an opportunity to think through the most obvious and most challenging questions and to provide just enough information to satisfy the individual(s) asking. Put yourself in the shoes of your stakeholders and think through the worst-case scenario of what they could ask.

Consider every possible angle and answer questions in the most straightforward and diplomatic manner possible without providing information that will only make the individual want to ask more questions.

In the scenario described above in which the CFO confessed to embezzlement, the Q&A might include:

Q: What happened?
A: *[The CFO] has been terminated.*

Q: Why was he terminated?
A: *He confessed to embezzling funds over the past year.*

Q: How did he manage to steal the money without anyone noticing?
A: *Forensic accountants found that he transferred money from our cash reserves to a defunct company account and then to his personal account.*

Q: How much did [the CFO] steal?
A: *Six hundred thousand dollars.*

In some instances, answers might read as similar or even redundant since they'll likely share similar phrasing. However, consider that (a) not every question on your list will be asked and (b) you don't want to give the impression that you shift positions or adapt your answers depending on the person or group asking the question. Messaging should remain consistent.

Meeting Scripts

Whether in outline or narrative form, a script provides guardrails and keeps the presenter(s) on message. It prevents them from unintentionally skipping over critical points or being knocked off track by questions from the audience. The content of the remarks, like other crisis communications, should convey that leadership is in control and is planning for every contingency.

The language for group meetings should be written in a conversational style and delivered confidently. If the speaker appears overwhelmed by the moment or demonstrates a lack of conviction, those gathered could quickly lose confidence.

As we'll see in the next chapter, the same goes for tone. Too cool and clinical might seem insensitive at times. But, on the other hand, being too emotional might undermine the message in a different situation.

A script for such a workplace gathering on the CFO embezzlement issue could be:

Thank you all for being here today.

As you are all valued members of our team, I felt obligated to share some news and to let you know what we are doing to address it.

After discovering missing funds and retaining an outside accounting firm to investigate, we have determined that our former CFO was embezzling from the company over the past year. We have terminated him and referred the matter to the district attorney's office.

We want to assure you that [the company] remains financially strong and, as you know, we've continued to expand. Last quarter saw record profits, and we could not have done it without all of you.

While we're deeply disappointed and feel a sense of betrayal at what has occurred, this does not impact who we are or our ability to serve our customers.

We're grateful for our board's support, and we have completely restructured our financial reporting and monitoring procedures to ensure this never happens again.

Does anyone have questions?

DEBRIEF

Post crisis, assemble your team of decision makers to review what went right and what needs to be improved upon. Learning from mistakes and making improvements to the plan where necessary ensures resiliency and the ability to bounce back from an interruption, big or small.

Go around the table, literally or virtually, and solicit input from everyone. Foster a safe space that's nonjudgmental and encourage folks to be self-critical. The goal should be to learn from the event, not to blame anyone for missteps, as the most honest feedback and candid insight can help prevent the same mistake(s) from being made twice.

These meetings, sometimes referred to as "postmortems," can help identify issues with your crisis plan. I recommend that it include, at the very least:

- a crisis response team

- crisis response protocols

- media procedures

- template statements

Depending on the size of your organization and the complexity of the issue you're confronting, planning might consist of a single meeting or a weekslong process. The crisis commandment "Anticipate What's Next," discussed in chapter 3, will ensure that you have anticipated every potential issue, question, and blind spot. Serving as a powerful reminder are the elements and tools reviewed in this chapter:

- the overall strategy

- key audiences

- timeline

- if-then scenarios

Last, but most certainly not least, are the necessary communications. The list of those to be delivered in written form or orally, should they be necessary, include:

- community letters

- media statements

- talking points

- Q&As

- meeting scripts

During a chaotic and fast-moving situation, you'd be surprised at how urgently messages need to be shared. In the case of an industrial accident, for instance, a range of stakeholders, from employees to clients to subcontractors to regulators, will want to know what happened *even before* you have a chance to start communicating. Plan accordingly.

6

SEVEN QUALITIES OF QUALITY COMMUNICATIONS

SAFEGUARDING YOUR REPUTATION CAPITAL is, first, the result of action you take and, second, the way you communicate that action. Even if a crisis is being managed expertly behind the scenes, panic can ensue if those mitigation efforts are not shared promptly with those who need to know.

To be an effective communicator, it's often necessary to simultaneously strike several different tones. How much of one and how little of another is necessary depends on the nature of the crisis and what information constituents will require to feel confident in the response. For instance, if a letter sent to customers about a product recall sounds genuine, but no actions to solve the crisis are shared, the brand won't come across as proactive, and stakeholders won't have much confidence that the issue is being addressed urgently.

Consider which of the following qualities your brand may need to reflect. Additionally, I've suggested some keywords to use in communications when trying to convey that particular quality or trait.

1. Competency

Whether an individual sits atop a Fortune 100 or a small nonprofit, subject matter expertise and strong leadership skills, including communicating, are among the most crucial elements to their success. The last thing anyone wants is a CEO, president, or executive director who is viewed as merely a puppet of the board of directors.

No one is immune from a crisis. What you say and *how* you say it in responding to the crisis is what sticks with people, and it either bolsters or bankrupts your reputation capital. Business students today are still taught the masterful crisis management demonstrated by Johnson & Johnson back in 1982, after the deaths of seven individuals who unknowingly ingested cyanide-laced Tylenol. It was the company immediately pulling the pain reliever from shelves, aggressively using advertising and the media to alert consumers, and quickly inventing tamper-proof pills and bottles that made the whole episode the definitive case study on how to regain the public's trust in the wake of a catastrophe.

On the flip side, Exxon is still judged harshly and remains the butt of jokes for its mishandling of a massive oil spill in 1989. Two hundred fifty thousand barrels spilled into Prince William Sound after the *Exxon Valdez* tanker ran aground off Alaska.[1] The company moved too slowly to contain the flow of oil into the sound, and it took leadership a week to issue a statement. Only after he was essentially shamed into it did the company's chairman travel to Alaska to witness the devastating environmental impact firsthand.

Most crises present some level of ambiguity. Quick and decisive action can cut through a perception of indecisiveness.

> KEYWORDS TO CONSIDER
> **experience, expertise, determine, decision, proactive**

2. Authenticity

Arguably, this is the most critical tone a brand needs to reflect when its reputation is under attack. The public can forgive a leader who isn't the most skilled communicator if they're perceived as telling the truth. Although I rarely counsel clients to say absolutely *nothing* in response to a crisis, keeping silent would be a smarter move than issuing a statement that projects as hollow, insincere, and smarmy, one that sounds as if you're only lip-syncing the words because legal counsel forced you to.

Sounding self-congratulatory is a missed opportunity to build on the trust and respect your brand has presumably built up over the years. Even when mounting a robust defense against an allegation that has no merit, the tone of communications should remain confident but humble. Gloating is never a good look and can only have negative repercussions.

Today's consumers are savvy and sophisticated; they can tell when a business is projecting, deflecting, or just going through the motions. They also demonstrate loyalty, not just to those products or services they value, but to brands that speak up about the issues they care about most.

This doesn't mean, however, that a leader should bare their soul in every communication. To quote a *Harvard Business Review* piece titled "The Authenticity Paradox," "disclosing every single thought and feeling —is both unrealistic and risky."[2] The author states that an unnecessary level of transparency can cause constituents to lose trust in a leader's ability to successfully navigate a situation or crisis.

> KEYWORDS TO CONSIDER
> **sincere, hopeful, appreciate, believe, intention**

3. Empathy

It's critical to try and understand and appreciate the situation from the other party's perspective. This is especially the case when an event or issue is responsible for the suffering of an individual or group. When thinking through written statements or preparing for sit-down interviews with reporters, consider how to humanize your brand and avoid language that might portray the organization as an entity that cares more about profits than people.

When projecting empathy, be careful not to sound or look as if you're merely going through the motions. For example, "thoughts and prayers" has been uttered by so many lawmakers and other VIPs in response to a tragedy or crisis that its overuse has made the phrase a hollow gesture. It's no longer considered authentic or truly empathetic, although it might have been at one time. Instead, it's now perceived as a lazy pro forma statement that offers no real response or solution.

According to CNN, "The devolution of 'thoughts and prayers'–like sentiment has been years in the making. The further it's embedded in our post-tragedy lexicon, the more it's mocked as a form of civilian slacktivism, and more recently as a form of political obfuscation."[5]

Utilize messaging that acknowledges the worries or fears your constituents might be feeling. If circumstances on the ground change and there are new concerns, recognize this and revise your language accordingly.

> KEYWORDS TO CONSIDER
> **understand, value, sympathize, relate, realize**

4. Trustworthiness

Delivering difficult news in a straightforward manner conveys honesty and integrity. This also means ensuring consistent messaging across audiences. If you can't establish yourself as *the* reliable go-to source of your own information, expect people to judge your brand harshly: at best, disorganized and incapable of managing your own problems and, at worst, disingenuous and intentionally misleading.

Remember: Trust is earned through time and hard work, not with a snap of your fingers. The opinion consumers hold about a brand typically depends on how much reputation capital it's earned up to that point. For instance, if a brand doesn't typically engage with followers on social media, don't assume it'll be able to start doing so once it's in crisis mode. It takes time and a deliberate strategy to build a following. This also includes sharing content that's consistent and on-brand with your mission.

> KEYWORDS TO CONSIDER
> **earn, promise, ensure, commit, guarantee**

5. Proactiveness

Be prepared and plan for threats before they happen. Once in crisis mode, get ahead of the questions you anticipate will be asked. Then, define the narrative and describe what you're doing to address the situation to ensure it never happens again. Once your version of events has been wrestled away by the press, a competitor, or a disgruntled member of your own community, you'll spend unnecessary hours on cleaning up a mess that could easily have been prevented.

In the chaotic moments following a crisis, rumors and misinformation can spread quickly. Ensure stakeholders have a clear and accurate picture of what occurred. For example, in the event of a fire at a downtown office building, news outlets will often report what first responders and eyewitnesses post on social media. Monitor these channels closely. In the event of an error, consider reaching out to the reporter or editor and having them correct their stories.

When crafting statements, be sure to share the information with those who'll be reading the communication will most want to know. For instance, in a cyber attack your audience will include customers whose data might have been exposed; in a construction accident on a new building, it will consist of those who live in neighboring properties.

> KEYWORDS TO CONSIDER
> **action, plan, prepare, strategy, ready**

6. Protectiveness

First and foremost, defend your hard-earned reputation. It's OK to circle the wagons, but don't adopt a bunker mentality in which vital information isn't shared, the brand "lawyers up," and communications include defensive and self-righteous language. Again, it's how you respond that will define the episode and, potentially, your legacy.

For example, if an employee is accused of committing a serious crime, a brand's messaging around the issue should include how it conducts thorough screening and background checks on all prospective employees. Understand that when the judgment or character of one employee is called into question, the situation might require defending the reputation of your entire workforce and detailing what due diligence is performed during the hiring process.

Keep in mind that being *protective* does not equate with taking an issue or criticism of that issue personally. Try to review communications as dispassionately as possible. Keep any hurt feelings or bruised egos from influencing how you make your case. This is where third-party counsel can be especially helpful to reality-check the tone of communications.

> KEYWORDS TO CONSIDER
> **insist, defend, uphold, safety, security**

7. Transparency

Heed the well-worn expression "Sunshine is the best disinfectant." Don't try to cover up certain details when they're an integral piece of the issue at hand. This information *always* comes to light in the end. It's better to rip the Band-Aid off and be forthcoming about what took place, even if some form of mismanagement or oversight was primarily responsible. The faster you come clean, the sooner you can make amends and move past it.

I've warned against oversharing, but equally important is not sounding as if you're holding back or cherry-picking facts to portray your brand in a more positive light. If the threat you're facing means a key audience is waiting for crucial information, the more transparent and helpful you are, the more likely your response and overall communication strategy will be viewed favorably.

KEYWORDS TO CONSIDER
open, cooperation, invite, explain, collaboration

DEBRIEF

Even if you speak in a manner that demonstrates all of the traits we've described, there will always be critics who could call you out, criticize you, and portray your organization as a bully picking on a much smaller adversary. Consumers are savvy and can discern when a brand is just paying them lip service. To review, the seven qualities you'll want to incorporate into your communications are:

- competency

- authenticity

- empathy

- trustworthiness

- proactiveness

- protectiveness

- transparency

To illustrate the practical application of these traits, what follows is an email alerting a school community (students, their parents, alumni, and donors) of an allegation of sexual abuse that allegedly took place on campus decades ago. See if you can spot how this communication reflects all seven qualities discussed.

Dear Friends:

Like you, all of us here on campus are troubled by the story which appeared on last night's Channel 6 newscast about a new allegation of sexual assault on campus more than four decades ago. You can be assured that we are committed to protecting the safety and security of all students in our care. We have consistently adapted our practices to keep our school safe and will continue doing so.

To be clear: In 1979, the then head of school immediately terminated the staff member after meeting with him about allegations he sexually assaulted a student. In addition, he reported the matter to the local police department and the state agency responsible for child protective services.

When new allegations recently surfaced about this former staff member and another student, we immediately retained a law firm with extensive experience in investigating such matters. As part of their investigation into misconduct that might have gone unreported at the time, we welcome anyone to come forward with information related to this issue.

We take this new allegation very seriously and are committed to discovering the truth of what may have occurred; we owe it to the individuals directly involved and to our community. Then, as now, we stand with all victims of sexual misconduct and recognize the courage it takes for them to come forward.

The lengths to which we go to protect our community are extensive. We require third-party training for our staff on how to properly interact with students, while always being mindful of appropriate boundaries and how to recognize predatory behavior. At all times, the safety and well-being of our students are our absolute top priority.

Please let me know if you have any further questions.

Sincerely,

[The Head of School]

Tone begins with word choice but can ultimately determine how constituents perceive a brand's personality. The nineteenth-century philosopher Friedrich Nietzsche is quoted as saying, "We often refuse to accept an idea merely because the tone of voice in which it has been expressed is unsympathetic to us."[4] This is human nature. Stakeholders receive and process information through their own unique lens.

7

THE CEO AS
SPOKESPERSON

YOUR ORGANIZATION is facing a serious threat. Its reputation—and perhaps its very existence—hangs in the balance. Having shepherded clients across sectors through countless issues, I've witnessed the time, energy, and resources it takes for leadership to respond effectively at these pivotal moments. While advance planning prepares the management team, the all-consuming nature of an unfolding crisis can easily derail their daily schedule.

Even if the CEO oversees or designates a senior team member to manage a crisis, the question of who should communicate to internal and external constituencies—to manage the *perception* of how a crisis is responded to—can be a topic of much debate. Just as there's no single strategy for responding to these urgent matters, a CEO's role in these moments of truth is nuanced and often dynamic.

CULTIVATING A STRONG COMMUNICATOR

One of the lessons I learned as a reporter who covered numerous corporate scandals is that not all CEOs are expert communicators. Even some of the most knowledgeable, business-savvy chief executives can struggle with speaking in a manner that adequately defends their brand when need be. The phrase "grace under pressure" is uttered so often it's become a cliché. Yet even the most skilled communicator can find themselves challenged by a chaotic, stressful set of circumstances.

The ability to maintain a sense of calm and control doesn't come naturally to most. How else do we explain incredibly smart and shrewd executives making a series of poor decisions when they're faced with a serious crisis? There's something about that moment, when the heat is turned up, that can lead otherwise intelligent, rational individuals to make the wrong call, become paralyzed by the pressure, or clam up in front of the press.

Before putting your CEO forward as the company spokesperson, here are some key considerations to think through ahead of time.

Relatability

Is your CEO capable of connecting and empathizing in a genuine way with those who may have been harmed? During any communications opportunity, the spokesperson should address their greatest fears, offer solutions, and make assurances to fix that which shouldn't have occurred. If the CEO cannot speak their language, either literally or figuratively, it might be best to go with someone who external constituencies can more easily relate to.

The often-cited example of a CEO who failed to empathize or relate is British Petroleum's Tony Hayward, who uttered, "I'd like my life back," during the Gulf of Mexico oil spill of 2010. The spill was the result of an explosion on the offshore drilling rig *Deepwater Horizon*. It didn't matter that he had issued a sincere apology right before those remarks, "We're sorry for the massive disruption it's caused their lives."[1]

Hayward issued a more full-throated apology the next day, but the damage was done. Coupled with images of the embattled CEO on board his sailboat off the coast of England weeks later, while the cleanup was still going strong in the Gulf, it was game over. Hayward was forced to resign the following month.

Timeliness

When there's a crisis in which the CEO must act as spokesperson, ensure they're seen and heard from at the appropriate moment(s). This may mean *as soon as possible*, but there are exceptions. For instance, if a crisis is escalating, it may make sense to hold the chief executive back until their words will have the greatest impact. It can be a tough needle to thread. If they wait too long to say something, it gives the appearance that the CEO was pressured or publicly shamed into commenting. In the public's eyes, a slow response often equals indifference.

In March of 2019, for example, Facebook was roundly criticized for its response, or lack thereof, to a hate-fueled gunman who used the social network to livestream his killing spree. The mosque attacks in Christchurch, New Zealand, left fifty-one people dead, yet it took two weeks for a Facebook representative to comment publicly. "Your silence is an insult to our grief," wrote the country's Privacy Commissioner John Edwards in a letter to Facebook executives.[2] At the very least, such a tragedy demanded an immediate expression of sympathy, plus a vow to review the platform's polices around live streaming.

DECISIVE ACTION, DECISIVE COMMUNICATIONS

In May 2021, Colonial Pipeline responded within an hour of learning it had been the victim of a cyberattack.[3] CEO Joseph Blount knew the fuel pipeline operator had to act immediately to isolate the ransomware and prevent it from spreading. He ordered a preemptive shutdown of the company's pipeline, which delivers almost half of the East Coast's fuel supply.

The company issued a statement that included, "Colonial Pipeline is taking steps to understand and resolve the issue. Our primary focus is the safe and efficient restoration of our service and our efforts to return to normal operation."[4]

Taking steps communicated that the company was wasting no time in getting on top of the situation. Realizing the move would spark panic buying at the pump, *normal operation* was the optimal phrase for those concerned about the ripple effect of a prolonged shutdown.

While there was a temporary spike in gas prices, it could've been a whole lot worse if Blount hadn't acted decisively. Such extreme measures are rarely popular in the moment, but considering Blount's limited options, the bold and difficult decision turned out to be the right call.

Expertise

If the CEO doesn't possess expert knowledge in the area at the heart of your brand's crisis, they should still be visible to acknowledge they're on top of the situation while allowing those with the technical know-how (a relevant department head or an on-site manager, for instance) to address the specifics of what happened and what steps are being taken to resolve the situation.

Sometimes, an informed third party is put forward, a strategy often referred to as "proxy communications." An example of *intentional* proxy communications is when federal agencies like the National Transportation Safety Board partners with an airline on the response to an aviation accident. They hold authority and credibility and possess a unique level of expertise to answer any questions about what may have caused the incident.

Then there's proxy communications born of out necessity to fill an information and communications vacuum. By the end of 2008, several salmonella cases and at least one death were linked to a processing plant belonging to the Peanut Corporation of America (PCA). Although PCA issued a recall of its products, it didn't provide a statement on the crisis until January 12, 2009. According to *Public Relations Review,*

> *PCA's lack of forthright communication allowed speculation,*
> *uncertainty, and anxiety about the peanut paste contamination*

to escalate. The corporation's reticence shifted the onus of respon-
sibility to peanut industry leaders and governmental agencies as
apprehensive consumers demanded information about the crisis.[5]

With PCA missing in action, the Centers for Disease Control and Prevention, the US Food and Drug Administration, health departments across several states, and peanut industry leaders like the Southern Peanut Farmers Federation stepped into the breach. They were able to inform the public about what type of products they should avoid eating, where the contaminated paste originated from, and the number of individuals who had fallen ill as a result.[6] In the end, the outbreak was responsible for nine deaths and thousands of consumers getting sick in what was one of the most extensive food recalls in US history.[7]

THE POWER OF THE PROXY

In 2015, executives at The Walt Disney Company responded immediately after an alligator killed a two-year-old boy by pulling him underwater at a Disney World lagoon in Orlando, Florida. Chairman Bob Iger, who was out of the country at the time, personally called the child's family to express his sympathy, while his top lieutenants released statements offering their condolences.

At the same time, a coordinated effort with the Florida Fish and Wildlife Conservation Commission helped deliver vital information to the press, who were staked out on the property. While Disney remained out front during this heartbreaking episode, wildlife experts provided additional background and investigation specifics: what the true alligator threat was in Florida, the reptile's behaviors that led to the tragedy, and what parents should do to protect their children. These are not topics on which Disney was qualified to answer on its own.

The theme park further managed the crisis by temporarily closing its beaches, building up the walls on all beachfront properties, and posting alligator warning signs. Already one of the most recognized and respected brands in the world, Disney's swift, responsive, and coordinated crisis response earned praise and prevented any lingering reputational damage.

Preparation

Just as an award-winning writer can benefit from a fresh set of eyes, so can the most prepared, well-spoken, and media-savvy executive benefit from regular crisis training. Such training takes time and commitment, often well before the skills are needed.

These exercises include being videotaped during mock interviews that can be played back and studied. Seeing themselves on camera can be revelatory for a CEO, who may have previously been unaware of areas in need of improvement, whether in style or substance. I'll talk more about these trainings coming up in the next section.

The public-facing responsibilities of a CEO will depend on the brand. But there's one thing you can count on: those who have built up some equity by engaging with the media and being visible before a crisis are typically given the benefit of the doubt in the tough times—at least at first.

Ensuring they're comfortable in the public eye helps a CEO achieve a certain level of confidence, even when crisis strikes. Part of our job as communications professionals is protecting and defending the organization and its leadership. So, when deciding who should be the spokesperson during a crisis, make sure the brand is putting its best foot forward.

A BRAND IN A TIGHT SPOT

In November 2013, when Lululemon founder and former CEO Chip Wilson appeared on *Bloomberg Insider*, he was asked about the quality of thousands of leggings that had to be recalled earlier in the year. His response is just as jaw-dropping now as it was then: "Some women's bodies just don't work for the pants."[8] In addition to Wilson essentially body-shaming Lululemon's loyal customer base, it was hard to fathom how his advisers had seemingly failed to prepare him for such an easily anticipated question.

He posted an apology on YouTube about a week later. Now, had he insisted his initial remarks were not very thoughtful or perhaps nothing more than a slip of the tongue, he might have nipped this crisis in the bud. Yet, it wasn't to be. The CEO claimed he was sad about the incident, which was a fine start, but never actually apologized to those he had offended with his hurtful remarks. Instead, he expressed sadness for Lululemon employees facing a backlash.

Least excusable of all? Playing the victim in the middle of a crisis you're solely responsible for. Wilson somehow managed both to be careless and to portray his company as the victim, blaming consumers for the brand's problems.

LEVELING UP: PRACTICE, PRACTICE, PRACTICE

Even if the chief executive doesn't possess the qualities discussed above, that doesn't mean they can't become a better communicator with proper instruction and practice. To quote a *Los Angeles Times* piece on the Utah mine collapse discussed earlier, "The news media will demand immediate answers. Critics will criticize. And CEOs need training to resist the urge to argue or speculate in times of great stress."[9] Here are some of the trainings that should regularly appear on the CEO's calendar.

Media Training

I would never recommend that a spokesperson speak to a journalist without feeling comfortable and confident in delivering a clearly articulated and vetted set of key messages—the information they most want to share during the interview. As with any skill, proficiency typically only comes after hours and hours of practice.

Anyone who could conceivably act as a brand spokesperson should undergo media training. Perhaps the trainee is someone who's never engaged with the press before and is unfamiliar with how journalists operate, what their priorities are, or the internal and external pressures they face. That's why the first part of the training should focus on the basics: the current media landscape, which topics and issues are considered newsworthy, and how stories across platforms and mediums (print, online, and broadcast) are written or produced.

For instance, we remind participants that, aside from a live or live-to-tape appearance (such as a podcast or an on-set television interview), the questions asked will typically not appear in the final story. This might seem obvious to those who regularly consume news. Still, it's an important reminder that helps participants understand the best way to construct their answers to prevent them from being misunderstood or taken out of context.

A strong answer can be conveyed in a few sentences, organized into three simple parts: your initial answer, backed up by *hard* or *soft* proof, and then a concluding statement that reiterates the first line of your response.

THE ABCs OF HOW TO ANSWER A QUESTION

Question: You recently fired a top manager, but only after several allegations of sexual harassment that date back more than a year. Can you assure us that leadership doesn't tolerate this type of that behavior?

Answer: I can assure you, as I have assured our employees and customers, that any harassing or bullying behavior that impacts our colleagues' mental health and well-being will not be tolerated.

Backup: What we determined in this case was that there was an issue with how complaints were filed and elevated within the company. Since this discovery, we've addressed that issue. In addition, we have instituted mandatory anti-harassment training. All employees are required to sign a new policy in which they pledge not to engage in such behavior and speak up when they do see it.

Conclusion: The termination of the former manager, along with all the new safeguards we have put in place, should communicate to all our stakeholders that we are serious about having a workplace free of harassment.

Another example:

Question: You just reported that the personal information of over two million customers was exposed in a data breach that took place over five weeks. What are you doing to respond?

Answer: Our entire team, including our chief technology officer, along with our outside cybersecurity firm, have been working around the clock since this breach was discovered.

Backup: First, I want to apologize to our customers who entrust us with their personal data. Despite having robust security in place, the breach occurred. Second, let me tell you what we've already done in response. We moved quickly to stop the data leak, and we've put new security technology in place, which we are currently testing. We're offering free credit reporting for our customers for up to one year, and we've established a hotline to answer any questions our customers may have.

Conclusion: We will do whatever is necessary to protect our intellectual property and our customers' privacy. That's a promise.

Within answers, transitional phrases allow the spokesperson to pivot from the initial response to the core messaging. This technique is executed consistently on Sunday-morning public affairs shows as guests debate matters of policy or politics. Common phrases include "It's important to understand that . . . ," "Keep in mind that . . . ," "What no one is asking is . . . ." To become proficient at using these techniques so as not to sound like they're avoiding the question, a spokesperson must practice regularly to hone their craft.

Mock Interviews

The most instructive part of the session is typically the mock interview, where the trainer plays reporter and asks the participant questions they might face in an actual exchange with a journalist. We position two chairs across from each other to mimic such a scenario. Recording this exercise on video allows the trainer to play it back for the spokesperson, provide constructive feedback, and point out what was done well and what can be improved upon.

While it's painful for some trainees to watch themselves on camera, it's only by doing so that many notice certain elements such as facial expressions, posture, or the content of their answers. For example, some individuals notice they repeatedly use phrases like "as such" or "at the end of the day" in every answer. Others will pick up on their nonverbal communication, like how they swivel when sitting in a chair or how they nervously tap their hand on their thigh. After these instant replays, we run through the mock interview a second and perhaps even a third time so the spokesperson can incorporate the feedback provided.

CRISIS ROLE-PLAYING

While the spokesperson will be front and center in a crisis, behind the scenes there will be multiple individuals working to respond to an emergency. Therefore, certain preparedness drills should be routinely held for the core crisis response team members so their roles and responsibilities are clearly defined.

Tabletop Exercises

After drafting a crisis plan, communications professionals should meet with their colleagues on the internal team to walk them through the procedures, answer any questions, and solicit their input for any edits or revisions that might be useful. This roundtable should include a discussion-based exercise where outside consultants or the in-house communications team act as facilitators and run the team through a simulated crisis. These tabletops help ensure that response procedures and communications protocols, as drafted, are practical. They help identify gaps in the chain of command as well as vulnerabilities that may not have been accounted for.

The trainer or co-trainers will have made notes, ahead of time, with all the conceivable twists and turns the hypothetical crisis could take, simulating the chaos of an actual reputational threat. After reading each of these developments aloud, they will ask questions of the participants to draw out responses and force the kind of real-time decision-making that occurs during an actual emergency. Participation by each team member should be encouraged, even if wrong answers might be provided. Tabletops are a crisis laboratory in many respects, a safe space to brainstorm and troubleshoot effective responses.

When my colleagues and I run these exercises, we like to take clients through at least two separate scenarios so they can practice responding to both a sudden crisis event that might involve first responders (e.g., an office fire or bomb threat) and a slower-moving reputational threat (e.g., executive fraud or a data breach).

Regulated industries such as transportation, energy, and health care are examples of sectors that require more robust crisis planning than most. For many big-city hospitals, for example, crisis simulations are federally funded and go far beyond sitting around a table. In fact, with little or no warning, a hospital will announce a disaster drill, and the staff must respond as if reacting to a real event. Many doctors in Boston credited these exercises for preparing them for the Boston Marathon bombing, when those patients rushed to area hospitals were suffering from battlefield-type injuries.

ARE WE WIRED FOR CRISIS?

I described crisis training, including tabletops, to my friend Rick, a PhD and practicing psychologist. He replied that it sounds very much like stress inoculation therapy (SIT). SIT is defined as "a psychotherapy method intended to help patients prepare themselves in advance to handle stressful events successfully and with a minimum of upset."[10] This method involves exposing an individual to small doses of stress during training, helping them learn how to regulate their emotions.

Rick described it to me this way: We all deal with stress differently. Our coping mechanisms are rooted in personality (nature), the environment in which we're raised (nurture), life experiences (learned behavior), or some combination of the three. Some of the stress responses we turn to are understandable and developmentally appropriate when we're younger, like sticking your fingers in your ears or closing your eyes. But as we grow and mature, strategies like these are no longer practical or adaptive in difficult situations.

Like psychological fault lines, our vulnerabilities or old, outdated tendencies can crack under pressure. The fight-or-flight response can kick in, clouding our judgment and rendering us unable to see several steps ahead—an invaluable trait when navigating any complex set of circumstances. Like any of us, those in the C-suite can fall victim to this. Exercises like media training and tabletops are designed to help leaders avoid that pitfall.

DEBRIEF

You should weigh many factors when determining whether the CEO should act as a spokesperson. These include the individual's comfort and confidence serving as the public face of the brand and the nature of the unfolding crisis. You'll want to consider:

- relatability (of the CEO)

- timeliness (should the CEO be deployed as a spokesperson right away or held back for the most critical moments?)

- expertise (on the subject matter at the heart of the crisis)

- preparation (have they been sufficiently trained to handle such high-pressure moments?)

Trainings and practice can make all the difference, whether the chief executive is a natural and outgoing communicator or has a more reserved personality. Some leaders may try and slough off trainings, insisting they're prepared. Remind them: just as an award-winning writer can benefit from another set of eyes, so can the most prepared, well-spoken, and media-savvy executive benefit from:

- media training

- mock interviews

- tabletop exercises

The important thing to remember when choosing a spokesperson is that you don't have to rely on the CEO alone. The chief executive can be one of several spokespeople. In fact, it will be necessary if the crisis is a 24/7 situation or is spread over a wide geographical area. For example, during the Gulf oil spill, BP leveraged several spokespeople—not just CEO Tony Hayward—out of sheer necessity.

When it comes to deciding who should be the public face of a brand during a crisis, make sure you're operating from a position of strength. This means having your CEO and other spokespeople prepared to take the heat when the spotlight on your brand is at its brightest.

8

MEDIA MATTERS
THE PRESS AS YOUR ALLY

IN HIS 2018 COLUMN "'No comment': The Death of Business Reporting," *Washington Post* columnist Steven Pearlstein decries the current state of media relations among large corporate brands. The piece makes the case that today's corporations view any engagement with the press with a jaundiced eye because of a lack of trust and the perception of too much risk.[1]

The risk argument is that even a slightly negative story can attract significant attention and have greater repercussions than ever before, so why even take the chance of speaking with a reporter? This holds especially true now that a brand has the option of speaking directly to the consumer through a multitude of its own channels, including its website, social media, email, and, of course, paid advertising.

The *trust* issue is more complex, and it's at the root of why corporate media relations has largely become a game of defense. Among the reasons for a loss of trust: demonization of the press by lawmakers, perhaps a past negative story or two about the business, and widespread newsroom layoffs (often resulting in a dissolution of the beat system), which has led to a lack of familiarity with reporters who may not cover an industry full time.

Yet leaders who recognize the press as a conduit and can engage reporters to disseminate important information are often more successful in achieving their external communications goals. Being willing to speak with journalists in both good and bad times creates a mutually beneficial two-way channel. They'll be familiar with the brand and the personalities who'll be on the other end of the line in the event they ever want or need to reach out.

If a reporter believes their contact at that brand is a straight shooter, it creates trust and understanding. Conversely, leaders who become combative and defiant with the press often become the story, compound the negative attention they may already be receiving, and prolong the headlines that could've otherwise been contained to a shorter news cycle.

FLIPPING THE SCRIPT

I've worked with hundreds of reporters across television, radio, and online platforms. Not all share the same motivations, ethics, or goals, but they do share many of the same professional instincts, or "news sense." This inner compass, often cultivated at a prestigious journalism school or on the job, enables a reporter to zero in on the most critical information, whether the story is about a local school committee meeting, a political campaign, or a brand in crisis.

As a local and network news reporter, I conducted thousands of interviews over nearly two decades. My focus was on asking smart questions, giving the interviewee a chance to explain or defend their position, and ensuring I held them to account for what they or their organization had done or were accused of doing. It was only *after* I made the leap into strategic and crisis communications, however, that I fully appreciated the amount of work put in by spokespeople to ensure they were prepared for that moment.

Conventional wisdom is that the interviewer plays offense while the interviewee is on defense. I train our clients to flip that script. As former US secretary of state Henry Kissinger quipped to the media, "What questions do you have for my answers?"[2] Kissinger had a job to do: deliver the administration's talking points for the day. Regardless of the question, he was going to do just that. Similarly, a spokesperson should think of an interview as playing offense: pushing out the brand's key messages in the context of answering a reporter's question(s).

Those at the head of a business, nonprofit, or any brand will be better equipped to protect their reputation if they're a regular consumer of news themselves. Even a basic understanding of what the media deems newsworthy and how they tell a story instills a greater awareness of how to respond appropriately to issues with a public-facing element. Having media-friendly language on stand-by describing what your brand does, what its mission is, and where it stands on important issues (in addition to the template statements we've covered) will put you one step ahead when a reporter comes calling.

Here's some additional insight into the media landscape and how reporters operate.

Reporters Believe They're Entitled to Information

If a spokesperson agrees to an interview, they shouldn't assume specific questions or topics are off-limits unless explicitly agreed upon ahead of time. This is just one reason to never skimp on preparation. If a spokesperson is adequately trained to pivot or bridge back to what they want to talk about, there shouldn't be any question they can't confidently field. In preparing ahead of these opportunities, communications pros shouldn't be afraid to get aggressive when playing reporter in a mock interview. Yes, the spokesperson they're working with may get slightly annoyed, but they'll thank them after that hard work pays off.

Reporters Won't Stop Until You Respond

Dodging a reporter's phone call or email is rarely a smart move. Would you rather respond or have the reporter show up unannounced at your office? Returning a journalist's calls or emails will help you get a handle on potential questions, the other people they're talking to, and their deadline.

In many cases, simply letting them know you'll call back can buy valuable time to formulate a plan or loop in others on the crisis response team.

You don't have to provide a full-fledged interview. Even a brief written statement will satisfy the reporter's query and, more importantly, the public's desire for a response. Again, "no comment" is a comment, one that communicates "I can't be bothered," "I don't have a good excuse," or "I'm guilty."

Reporters Have Limited Time to Digest Information

When I was a local news reporter working the day shift, I often had to file stories for the noon, 5 p.m., and 6 p.m. newscasts. Add social media posting responsibilities on top of that, and there's next to no downtime for today's journalists. Some interviews might last only a couple of minutes. So keep this in mind and plan to get your most important points across at the top of a statement or interview in clear, succinct language.

"Burying the lead" is a news industry term for putting an essential part of the story below less critical information. It's also important for corporate spokespeople to never bury the lead. That means covering the most crucial information in your first few answers. As the interview may not last long, never think you can save your best for last.

Reporters Might Need Background

Not every journalist possesses a firm grasp of the business or industry they're covering on a particular day. "General assignment" reporters may very well have been covering a car crash or bank robbery just an hour before covering a brand in crisis. Whenever possible, spokespeople should take a few minutes prior to the interview to provide some background and context, especially if it involves a subject matter the reporter will need to be educated on to accurately write their story.

At the end of the interview, a reporter will often ask, "Is there anything else you would like to add?" Many people view this question as a throwaway, something the reporter does merely as a courtesy. Don't pass it up. It's a real opportunity to deliver or reiterate critical messages, and it might just end up being the sound bite or quote used in the story. It can be especially effective to use a *flag* phrase such as "The thing that's really important to remember . . ." or "The key point here is. . . . " Finish by asking the reporter if there's anything they need further explained, and make yourself available by email or phone to answer any additional questions before they file their story.

Reporters May Need Follow-Up

The silver lining of outlets now posting stories online hours and, sometimes, days before they appear in the print version is that there's more time to push for corrections or edits. With content being posted more frequently, there tend to be more errors, factually and grammatically, making it online than ever before. This has created a whole new step in the process: one that might be referred to as the "cleanup" stage of reporter outreach.

While it's essential to respond quickly in a crisis, it's just as important to be accurate; ensure that statements contain confirmed information that doesn't have to be walked back after sharing. If important facts aren't available yet, admit as much and say you'll provide an update as soon as possible. Readers will appreciate your straightforward approach and commitment to providing up-to-date information.

THE SPOKESPERSON'S CHECKLIST

Most crisis responses begin with a written statement. This ability to have complete control over the message and the language used without having to answer any questions is the most efficient method of sharing a response and the one that entails the least amount of risk. A press conference or one-on-one interview with a reporter occurs only in a relatively small number of situations. Crises where a written statement might not be sufficient include those in which the public is at risk, lives have been lost, or a public figure is embroiled in scandal.

Another instance where you may want to speak with a reporter is if your initial statement has fallen flat or been widely misinterpreted and made matters even worse. A poorly worded statement has the power to compound the damage and ratchet up the pressure on leadership. One effective way to address negative coverage and turn the narrative around in your favor is to agree, after sufficient preparation, to a sit-down interview with a reporter *on the record.*

Typically, if an interview doesn't air right away, it's edited down in postproduction, leaving some room for negotiation after the sit-down. For instance, if you felt like something you said could be misconstrued by the viewing public, you can request that the reporter leave it out entirely or, at the very least, include the necessary context in an introduction, their narration of the story, or immediately after the story (known as the "tag"). The outcome of the request will depend both on the reporter and how integral the sound bite is to the story.

One downside of a taped interview is, again, that you can never be 100 percent certain that the best sound bites will be used and that something you said won't be taken out of context. That's why some corporate spokespeople prefer live interviews. While there might be more pressure to perform, the viewers see everything, including the spokesperson responding to every claim or allegation.

If you do decide to go *on the record* with a reporter either over the phone for a print story or on a live broadcast, you should have certain expectations at the outset. Planning for these rules of engagement ahead of what could be a contentious interview will help you remain on point.

Anticipate and Practice Answering the Tough Questions

Like swinging two bats in the on-deck circle, repeatedly preparing for "gotcha" questions will make answering the more routine ones easier. This assuredness is apparent in how direct a person is when speaking, the content of their answers, even their body language. When you watch a spokesperson who's a true pro, their demeanor is consistent across the interview and isn't dependent on the difficulty of the question asked. Remember, it all begins with your key messages and the ability to effectively pivot. As I discussed in the section on media training, transitional phrases allow the spokesperson to shift from the initial response to their most important and well-rehearsed talking points.

Assign a Level of Importance to Facts

This includes false assumptions by the interviewer. If you disagree with the premise of the question, begin your answer with that assertion. Without getting adversarial, it's the spokesperson's job to highlight the key issues, so don't let the press wrestle the storyline away from you. Remember, it's your story to tell.

Don't let the reporter put words in your mouth. Quotes and sound bites can be selectively edited afterward, so don't give up any ground in the battle to defend your reputation. This includes turning negative questions into positive answers.

For example, if the question is:

Isn't it true that your organization is guilty of mismanagement?

Instead of:

It isn't true that our organization is guilty of mismanagement.

. . . the answer should be:

Our organization is managed properly at all times.

Be Concise

This is a point I've made often about drafting crisis communications. It's no different when speaking in a high-stakes interview. Discipline is paramount when there's little margin for error. Although you'll want to go on the offensive, the more you say, the more likely you could end up saying something that doesn't effectively make your point or that you might even end up regretting. So, resist the temptation to expound beyond what's necessary. Instead, keep answers tight and focused on what it is you want to get across.

REPORTING: TRICKS OF THE TRADE

Reporters will use numerous techniques to draw out the most revealing information and insight possible. Here's the inside scoop on some tactics reporters often employ, along with how you can leverage them to defend your brand.

Expect a Reporter to Use Small Talk

No matter how friendly or disarming a reporter might seem, never let down your guard. Nothing is wrong with a little polite chitchat. You may even discover that you have friends in common or enjoy the same restaurant. But never lose sight of the task at hand. The reporter isn't your friend, especially during a crisis; avoid getting lulled into a false sense of security. Know that anything you say could end up in the story, even if the video camera or voice recorder is not rolling.

Expect a Reporter to Ask the Same Question in Multiple Ways

Recognize that if a reporter doesn't get what they want out of your answer the first time, they'll ask the same question again, only phrased differently. It isn't incumbent upon the spokesperson, however, to answer any differently. Especially with a question designed to portray the organization in a negative light, you should feel empowered to answer, "I believe I've answered that question already," when asked a second time. This is a polite way of signaling to the reporter that you've said all you have to say on the topic, and it's time to move on.

Expect a Reporter to Begin a Question with "Some Might Say . . ."

This expression lends legitimacy to the premise of a reporter's question. Or at least they think it does. In reality, it's lazy and reflects a lack of preparation on their part. When this occurs, you have every right to ask who "some" are. Don't accept the premise of a question if you believe it's based on hyperbole or inaccurate information. Additionally, don't be afraid to ask the reporter a question if it helps you better understand what it is they're asking. Phrased properly, it won't be considered combative or rude.

Expect a Reporter to Try to Use Silence against You

Most interview subjects anticipate a reporter will, at some point, interrupt their answer with another question. If that interruption never comes, the individual often continues talking. Don't feel like you need to fill the silence in between finishing the answer and the next question being asked just to be polite. This is often when the "gotcha" moments happen or where major faux pas can occur. The more one talks, the more likely they are to say something they regret. Reporters need their subjects to reveal compelling details, and they know silence makes most of us uncomfortable. Don't take the bait. "Embrace the silence," we advise our clients. This means not going off on a tangent just because you think the interview is going well and making points that are not central to the message.

Expect a Reporter to Get Up Close and Personal

Whether sitting or standing, or whether the crew is using a traditional "stick" microphone or a wireless lavalier that clips onto your lapel or collar, anticipate that you'll be close to the reporter, sometimes with only inches of space between you. This setup can be jarring for many, especially if it isn't what they envisioned. I shared a story in the introduction of a client who was baffled when I set up my chair so close to hers in a mock interview that our knees were practically touching, only to thank me after the journalist did just that in the actual interview. Investigative reporters, especially, will use these tight quarters to turn up the heat on their interview subjects.

DEBRIEF

Before agreeing to do an interview or even issuing a statement, research the reporter, the outlet, and their past stories. What subjects are they typically writing about? Have they demonstrated bias when writing about the topic the spokesperson will be speaking with them about?

Each reporter has their own distinct style. Yet, commonalities exist when it comes to how most go about their job:

- Reporters believe they're entitled to information.

- Reporters won't stop until you respond.

- Reporters have limited time to digest information.

- Reporters might need background.

- Reporters may need follow-up.

When prepping a spokesperson for an actual interview, have them practice answering the tough questions, assign a level of importance to facts, and work on being concise. Each of these requires a good degree of self-discipline, as you likely won't know the specific questions that will be asked. Yet, you can anticipate the reporters will:

- use small talk

- ask the same question in multiple ways

- begin a question with "Some might say . . ."

- try to use silence against you

- get up close and personal

Good reporters do their homework. Spokespeople need to do the same. They're the subject matter experts, after all, and should hold the upper hand in an interview. It isn't enough to talk strategy with an inner circle of trusted advisers; professional media training and regular practice are key to ensuring the spokesperson is prepared and that the organization's reputation remains intact.

9

SOCIAL MEDIA AND THE RISE OF THE STAKEHOLDER

IN 2011, I WAS WRITING a story for broadcast about a 22-year-old woman named Molly Katchpole. She'd collected more than three hundred thousand signatures on a Change.org petition opposing a new five-dollar monthly fee introduced by Bank of America for customers to use their debit card.[1] It was just five bucks, but the backlash was emblematic of the consumer outrage toward financial institutions at the time expressed by the Occupy Wall Street movement. The grassroots campaign was fueled by social media and mainstream media coverage, and the bank capitulated after just a month, scrapping its plans for the fee. It was the moment I realized the tables had turned: by asserting its influence, an online community could level the playing field between a single consumer and the world's biggest brands.

POSTING PROFITABLY

With this new democratization of the corporation-consumer relationship, crisis response plans need to anticipate how to contain these issues and respond effectively across every channel. On social media, which stakeholders turn to in good times and bad, consider this advice before responding to user posts or comments calling out your brand:

Define a True Crisis

It's easy to overreact to a critical comment. Just keep in mind that a single post about, say, poor customer service is a concern, not a crisis. Even so, if leadership is used to only positive publicity, just one negative comment can throw the team for a loop. Be the voice of reason and don't let others lose perspective.

When setting up a social listening program, decide which metrics will be used to measure online conversations and then what level of activity constitutes a simmering issue or a full-blown crisis. Monitoring software such as Critical Mention or Nuvi weigh a combination of factors, including sentiment (positive, neutral, or negative) and whether the issue is trending up, down, or has plateaued. Is the social chatter from influencers with thousands of followers or just an online troll looking to stir up trouble?

Institute a Social Media Policy

When determining standards and practices for posting on the organization's official channels, be as specific as possible to account for a wide range of scenarios. What might be viewed as polarizing content will depend on the brand's identity and mission.

Although being bold or even risqué might be encouraged on social media, derogatory posts that evoke racial, ethnic, or religious stereotypes are examples of lines that should never be crossed.

Opinions vary on the extent to which an employer can enforce similar standards for their employees' own social media channels. But, at the very least, there should be a set of clear expectations and guidelines around privacy. This means not sharing confidential or sensitive work information. While an organization doesn't want to appear as if it's stifling anyone's freedom of expression, it's also impor-tant that employees appreciate that they are, in many ways, ambassadors of the brand.

A cautionary tale for employees is that of Jennifer Sey, a top executive at Levi Strauss, who left the company after she insisted she was denied a promotion to CEO because of her outspoken criticism on her personal Twitter account against school closures and mask mandates for children during the COVID-19 pandemic. According to the *New York Times*, "Ms. Sey's outspokenness drew criticism both inside and outside the company, including threats of boycotts. The tweets came when Levi's was using public health guidance to manage protocols across hundreds of stores and in distribution centers."[2]

Think before Posting

The expediency of social media is also its curse, so don't be an impulsive or emotional poster. Many crises have been sparked by posts shared before weighing the potential implications. Simply asking, "Who might take offense to this post or image?" will likely keep you out of hot water.

Yet how often do we hear about a brand's self-induced crisis after its media managers post content or comments intended to be funny, irreverent, or edgy but that completely miss the mark? You may recall:

- In 2014, retailer American Apparel posted an image to its Tumblr account celebrating July 4. Simple enough, one would think. Only the image the brand posted, which it thought was of a fireworks display, was an iconic photo of the 1986 Challenger space shuttle explosion.[3]

- After the 2017 Boston Marathon, sponsor Adidas sent a congratulatory email to runners that read: "Congrats, you've survived the Boston Marathon!" which recalled the deadly bombing at the event just four years earlier.[4]

- During the Arab Spring protests of 2011, fashion designer Kenneth Cole tweeted an out-of-touch and insensitive line promoting his clothing line's spring collection. It read, "Millions are in uproar in #Cairo. Rumor is they heard our new spring collection is now available online."[5]

In each instance, condemnation was swift, and the brands were forced to issue a public apology. Underscoring these heightened expectations around brand accountability, only 8 percent of US consumers in a recent survey said they'd remain silent if they saw inappropriate behavior from a brand on social media.[6]

Consider Who Is Talking

What is the profile of the user who is posting controversial or provocative comments about your brand? Are they a true influencer with tens or hundreds of thousands, perhaps even millions, of followers? This isn't to say that a single comment can't gain traction and go viral, but social media is all about eyeballs. If someone has ten followers on Twitter, their tweet about you is akin to the proverbial tree falling in a forest: no one is around to hear it.

To learn more about repeat critical posters, check to see if they have accounts on other social media channels. If they appear to be an internet troll, conspiracy theorist, or general troublemaker, know that trying to rationalize with them and appealing to their "common sense" will likely be an exercise in futility.

As these users feed off emotional—that is, angry—responses, it's important to answer their posts with factual statements if they're deserving of a response at all. Even a little bit of kindness will disarm a troll who isn't typically expecting such a comeback. If they persist in making inflammatory and false statements on your corporate channel, it's OK to block the individual in your privacy settings as a last resort.

Pause Unrelated Posts When Appropriate

If your organization is dealing with a crisis, evaluate whether you should be posting regularly scheduled content, some of which might have been planned a month or more in advance. Could followers view any imagery in poor taste in the context of current events? Be mindful of milestones on the calendar such as the anniversary of a tragedy that might be trending online to ensure the language you've chosen couldn't somehow be linked to that discussion and characterized as being in bad taste.

A few years back, a colleague and I worked with a university that was the subject of an unflattering exposé on network television. As timing would have it, an extensive fundraising campaign was set to kick off a day after the segment aired. This campaign would use the school's social media platforms to help raise awareness, and a phone bank run by current students would reach out to alumni for donations. We advised the institution to push the start date of the campaign to the following week. In the end, there was minimal online chatter about the news piece for a day or two, but it was better to be safe than sorry.

Take Conversations Offline

When responding to a complaint in a comment thread, answer once. If the poster comments again, tell them that you'd be happy to continue the conversation in a direct message where you can ask for a phone number or email address. This accomplishes the goal of being—and appearing—responsive to users following the thread, while requesting a one-on-one conversation to handle the complaint more personally.

If the poster rejects your offer to take the conversation offline, they're likely more interested in making a show than getting to the bottom of the issue. At that point, you've done all you can. Providing a customer service phone number or email is one way to end the conversation without appearing as if you're ignoring the individual.

ADDRESSING CONCERNS IN REAL TIME

Southwest Airlines has received many accolades over the years for its masterful use of social media and creative content to tell its brand story. At no time did this expertise pay off more than in the summer of 2016, when the airline experienced a widespread technology failure that lasted twelve hours. The outage led to the cancellation of 2,300 flights over four days, impacting as many as two hundred fifty thousand passengers.[7] The glitch took down Southwest's website and email, making its Facebook page and Twitter feed de facto customer service hotlines.

According to the *Dallas Morning News*, "Southwest received 90,000 inbound social media messages over the four days following the outage."[8] While the airline's social media team couldn't answer every single message, it responded frequently enough to ensure frustrated customers understood that Southwest was on top of the situation, working to resolve the glitch as quickly as it could.

The airline also produced and posted video updates to keep customers in the loop throughout the ordeal. It was over these channels that passengers received essential information such as how to book new flights or secure vouchers for overnight accommodations.[9]

Even for those brands with a fully staffed social media team to respond to posts in real time, deciding *when* and *how* to engage with posters during a crisis can be a daunting task. One of the most common questions we're asked by clients trying to prevent an issue from escalating on social media is, "Should we respond and, if so, how?"

Each situation should be evaluated on its own merits. Still, there are a number of guidelines my colleagues and I follow when offering counsel. Southwest's response to its 2016 crisis mirrors many of these recommendations. Let's take a closer look.

Consider responding when the poster makes a thoughtful comment or asks a question. Offering real-time responses and solutions signals a high level of accountability and a strong commitment to customer satisfaction. Even if information isn't available at the time to offer accurate answers or fixes, it's better to say the issue is being worked on than to say nothing at all. Consumers are forgiving if they know a business is acting in good faith to resolve the issue at hand.

If details in a developing situation aren't immediately known, brands can offer the stopgap statements I've discussed such as "We are aware of the situation and are still gathering more information" to bridge to when facts are available to share. If a specific course of action is promised in response to an issue or crisis, be prepared to back it up. Again, it's better to avoid walking back any promises made simply because they sounded good in the moment.

Early in the 2016 technology failure, for example, Southwest's posts included "We are aware and investigating current issues with our systems. We will keep you posted as we have more information to share" and "There's a tech issue we're working to resolve. Very sorry for the frustration. Thanks for bearing w/us."[10]

While plenty of customers made their frustrations known, there were a variety of positive responses, including:

- "Thanks for the head's up"

- "I know you guys are doing everything you can to fix this asap!! <3 yall!"

After one customer posted, "Waiting for someone to land & don't know if it is affecting departure times," Southwest provided clarity, responding, "Yes, departure times have been impacted. We have all hands on deck investigating and appreciate your patience."[11]

Consider responding when the poster offers constructive criticism. Recall the case of Whole Foods CEO John Mackey, who came around to a critic's point of view after months of research and reflection. While keyboard warriors are often looking for instant gratification, there might be lessons from which a brand can make improvements and benefit over the long term.

When tensions are running high, it's easy to become overly sensitive about even the smallest critique. Appreciate that feedback means someone cared enough to provide their opinion. View this as an opportunity to help your organization step up its game in a specific area where it might be vulnerable.

When someone tweeted, "really I wish you had told us this MANY HOURS ago," about the Southwest outage, the airline quickly replied, "We feel your frustrations & we're sorry for the inconvenience. We'll communicate updates when the site is fully functional."[12]

In an interview a week after the crisis, Southwest CEO Gary Kelly said he was confident that the company could learn lessons from the incident that would help the airline better recover during "future disruptions."[13]

Consider responding when the poster shows support. Try not to come off as self-congratulatory, aggrandizing, or exaggerating more than you've accomplished. If you still have work to do responding to or managing a situation, say so. Again, don't make any commitments or promises you cannot realistically keep. While it's nice to bask in the glow of a job well done, your customers might be back to give you hell the next day.

Even though it took some time for regular flight schedules to resume once Southwest's systems were restored, passengers were considerably more charitable with the friendly comments. When a passenger tweeted "fly safe" below the airline's most recent statement on Twitter, the social team responded, "We will, Rob. Have a good day!" The airline didn't reply to every compliment, including one that said, "Great job! You handled it with the kindness and professionalism we should expect from all companies."[14]

Consider NOT responding when the poster is only making derogatory remarks that might contain hyperbolic language and aren't focused on an issue you can fix. When someone is merely trolling your brand, there's little upside in engaging. I don't recommend deleting these comments, as this only tends to exacerbate the issue. However, you'll likely need to do so when the comments contain vulgar language or when personally hurtful remarks are made about someone in your organization.

For instance, during the Southwest crisis, there were plenty of tweets that the airline didn't respond to, including, "I don't care, just fix it" and "am more unhappy now after reading this BS. You are obviously NOT the best in the business! Our trip is now cancelled!"[15] The reality is that no response or apology from the airline's social media team would've satisfied those posters.

Consider NOT responding when a poster asks a rhetorical question where a response isn't expected. Instead, take the time to understand that individual's true intent and the point they were trying to make. If there's no immediate answer that will satisfy the poster, it's better not to respond. Any answer you provide could end up being critiqued even more harshly than your original post.

Southwest passengers dealing with canceled flights, lengthy and uncertain wait times, and delayed vacations got quite salty due to the chaos and uncertainty that ensued. Questions included, "Why board us when the system was down?" and "Are they going to delay my flight bc right now there's no chance of us getting on that plane if it leaves on time due to this."[16]

Consider NOT responding when a poster draws comparisons between your business and a competitor. Regardless of your reply, you'll only attract additional attention by making a statement that references another brand. Plus, those on social (and in traditional) media will take note, likely causing your reply to become a story of its own. Better to own the issue, take your lumps, and keep others out of it.

For instance, among the tweets Southwest never replied to were "as I sit at SFO & watch Delta, United, Virgin flights take off, I ask, how is it that Southwest can never get it together?" and "less tweeting, more fixing pls #FlyJetBlue #NeverSouthwest."[17]

DEBRIEF

Timeliness is vital when responding to a fast-moving crisis where a brand is being inundated with questions and complaints. Still, if the organization has planned properly, it can rely on those response protocols that have been put in place. If information, a solution, or a fix isn't readily available, say as much and promise to communicate as soon as it is. In the meantime, work to assuage concerns and answer questions to the extent possible.

The immediacy of social media is what makes it the perfect communications tool and one with plenty of risk as well. To avoid making mistakes, consider these recommendations:

- Define a true crisis.

- Institute a social media policy.

- Think before posting.

- Consider who is talking.

- Pause unrelated posts when appropriate.

- Take conversations offline.

My previous recommendations around tone of language apply to communicating on social media as well. Authenticity and accountability are perhaps most crucial in today's social ecosystem, where plenty of users are ready to pounce at the sight of any language that appears overly robotic or fake. Instead, customize and personalize preapproved language so it resonates as thoughtful with all who see it.

Case in point, the responses from Southwest's social media team such as "We're truly sorry we let you down," "We hear you," "So sorry to keep you waiting," and "We know this has been a difficult day" always seemed to hit the right notes.

To navigate a perilous online situation where your reputation is under assault, follow these rules of engagement:

Consider responding when a poster:

- makes a thoughtful comment or asks a question

- provides constructive criticism

- offers a positive or supportive comment

Consider NOT responding when a poster:

- is making only derogatory remarks

- asks a rhetorical question

- draws comparisons between you and a competitor

Large consumer-facing brands such as Southwest Airlines will have the social media infrastructure to view and reply to multiple posts in real time. Your brand may not. Still, by following some of the guidance offered in this chapter, posts that necessitate answers can be prioritized above the rest. Doing so will support an integrated crisis response with timely and thoughtful digital communications which will be watched and judged just as closely as the management of the crisis itself.

10

REPUTATION BY ASSOCIATION

IT WASN'T SO LONG AGO that higher education and cultural institutions such as museums, symphonies, and dance companies were the beneficiaries of trusting deference. Today, they're just as susceptible to public pressure as any brand is to act against alleged or confirmed wrongdoings or injustices. This is especially the case if they aren't already communicating about what they're doing to right a perceived wrong.

While symbolic, a college or university's acceptance of large monetary gifts and the bestowing of honorary degrees are not frivolous or insignificant gestures. Today, they're perceived as full-throated endorsements of the powerful VIPs the institutions are connected to as a result. Whether those individuals are businesspeople, entertainers, or academics, their personal crises have increasingly become crises for all the institutions they're affiliated with.

Although his conviction would be overturned in 2021 due to a legal technicality, legendary comedian Bill Cosby's conviction on sexual assault charges in April 2018 (in addition to being accused by dozens more women) was not just a reckoning for the legendary comedian. It was an inflection point for the institutions of higher education that had showered "the Cos" with honorary degrees over previous decades. Coinciding with the #MeToo movement, his alleged behavior could no longer be swept under the rug.

NAVIGATING UNCHARTED WATERS

Cosby had degrees bestowed upon him from at least sixty colleges and universities (including my own alma mater) looking to leverage an appearance by the iconic entertainer to burnish their own status.[1] Having earned the nickname "America's dad" when his eponymous sitcom *The Cosby Show* was at the height of its popularity in the 1980s, he was considered to be about as safe a choice as any public figure for such an honor. For the institution extending the invite, having Cosby address graduates guaranteed positive publicity.

The 2018 verdict left some of America's most prestigious institutions at a loss for what to do about their affiliation with Cosby. Higher education was already facing resounding calls for accountability around sexual misconduct. Activists have been emboldened by #MeToo, along with Title IX, a tool for student survivors of sexual violence to hold their schools accountable if they believe it mishandled their complaint. In the past, colleges and universities could skate by without commenting on the questionable character of a past honoree or donor. That's now ancient history.

While most schools were already doing everything they could to eliminate sexual misconduct from their campus, the ugliness of the Cosby ordeal required institutions to send the strongest message possible. As a result, dozens revoked Cosby's degree, along with issuing strongly worded statements condemning his crimes and reasserting a zero-tolerance policy toward any form of misconduct.

Still, the rationale for revoking an honor, returning a large donation, or removing a name from a building is a slippery slope. What, precisely, is the litmus test? Is it having broken specific laws? What if there's never a guilty verdict due to an out-of-court settlement? What if a judge throws out a case on a legal technicality, as Cosby's was in June 2021? What if the honoree didn't break any laws but made controversial statements about a hot-button issue such as race, politics, or immigration that are deemed offensive and are inconsistent with the institution's values?

Here are five dos and don'ts when weighing the impact of donor or honoree misconduct.

Don't Wait to Comment

If news breaks or information comes to light, don't wait for students to start a petition, donors to complain, or the media to call. It will take time to assess the situation and define a path forward. However, a statement expressing that the institution is troubled by developments and that new information will be considered at the next trustee or board meeting is one way of addressing an unknown issue that could have severe consequences for the community.

Avoid Definitive Statements at the Outset

In 2017, when first asked about their past honoring of Bill Cosby, Wesleyan University in Connecticut was one of a handful of schools that explicitly said it had a policy of not rescinding honorary degrees.[2] Rensselaer Polytechnic Institute in New York responded that it didn't have a mechanism for revoking degrees and historically had not done so.[3] George Washington University said, in 2015, that degrees are bestowed based on what is known about the individual at that time.[4] In the end, all three of those schools revoked Cosby's degree.

It's a good lesson that institutions should avoid communicating in such a way that they may have to walk back statements or policy positions. Consistency is critical. It demonstrates strong leadership and a set of values that aren't susceptible to a trend or fad.

Let the Community Have Its Say

An administration or board perceived as tone-deaf, insensitive, or aloof will only enrage those who want their voices heard. If the actual vote to revoke an honor or to return a sizable donation typically takes place behind closed doors, consider allowing public comment before the official decision, so key stakeholders feel as if they've had their say. Promise to keep the community updated and follow through. Consider each audience and what it needs to feel confident in how the institution handles the matter.

THE ART WORLD RESPONDS TO A DONOR CRISIS

In early 2018, the world learned the true scope of Purdue Pharmaceuticals' deceptive marketing practices. Purdue, the maker of OxyContin, was singled out by state attorneys general across the country for its role in the deadly opioid crisis.

Activist groups demanded that museums immediately cut ties with the Sackler family, owners of Purdue Pharma, who have donated millions of dollars to such institutions. A group of prestigious recipients including the National Portrait Gallery, the Tate Modern, and the Guggenheim agreed to stop accepting gifts from their longtime benefactors.

According to the *New York Times*, "The increased scrutiny on donors is forcing museums to navigate moral dilemmas and a political climate where a protest can go viral in a matter of hours. At the same time, they must mollify the wealthy benefactors who help keep the lights on and would rather not see their donations open them up to public examination."[5]

The Metropolitan Museum of Art, known as the Met, was also the target of protests. After a monthslong review of its gift policies, the museum announced it too would no longer accept gifts from the Sacklers.[6]

"There is also the difficult question of where to draw a line," said President Daniel Weiss: "We would only not accept gifts from people if it in some way challenges or is counter to the core mission of the institution, in exceptional cases. . . . The OxyContin crisis in this country is a legitimate and full-blown crisis."[7]

The Met, however, resisted removing the family's name from their glass-enclosed Sackler Wing, despite the demands of protesters. In October 2020, the museum announced that even that decision was under review after Purdue reached a $225 million settlement with authorities.[8] Finally, in December 2021 the name was removed as the Met severed all ties with the family.

Conduct an Independent Review

If an investigation is warranted, bring in an outside law firm with experience in such matters and without previous ties to the institution. This can be especially helpful in an environment in which some in leadership or on the board might be conflicted or could look to blame one another.

Promising that the organization will fully cooperate with investigators and that the findings will be shared (while maintaining confidentiality) communicates a high degree of transparency and accountability. In addition, investigators can provide guidelines for vetting prospective future donors and honorees, accepting gifts, and inviting prestigious individuals for speaking opportunities and other high-profile events.

In March 2019, the *New York Times* reported on alleged behavior by billionaire philanthropist Michael Steinhardt, whose name is on New York University's School of Education. The allegations of sexual harassment by half a dozen women who worked at nonprofits that benefited from Steinhardt's generosity rocked NYU. A prominent law firm was retained to investigate whether Steinhardt had engaged in inappropriate conduct with students, faculty, or staff.[9] Because it was found that none of his accusers were associated with the school, it was ultimately determined that his name would stay.[10]

Predictably, some in the NYU community were upset because they viewed the alleged behavior, wherever it may have taken place, as offensive and negatively impacting the public image of the school. Committing to an independent investigation along with a willingness to accept and act on its findings will go a long way toward getting community members and perhaps even key critics on board.

"Never Let a Good Crisis Go to Waste."

Use the opportunity as a catalyst for change and to reimagine an even better institution. Update policies and procedures around the selection and vetting of honorees and donors. Importantly, don't forget a process to revoke honorary degrees, rename buildings, and return donations.

Think through the infinite number of issues that might occur and consider including clauses in agreements referencing ongoing personal conduct, so expectations are clear.

DEBRIEF

Institutions are under no legal obligation to revoke a degree, return a donation, or remove a name from a campus building. Even so, they will very much be judged in the court of public opinion. Students, members, donors, alumni, and faculty, for instance, are quick to let colleges and universities know when they're offended by something their beloved institution has or has not done. To get ahead of your community and define the narrative,

- don't wait to comment

- avoid definitive statements at the outset

- let the community have its say

- conduct an independent review

- "never let a good crisis go to waste"

These decisions are high-stakes and, if not weighed carefully, they could set a dangerous precedent. An institution never wants to appear susceptible to a whim, a fad, or a passing fancy. For instance, if a university revokes an honor or a museum cuts ties with a wealthy donor, it shouldn't regret the decision five, ten, or even fifty years later.

11

COMMUNICATING
CULTURAL COMPETENCE

WE'RE LIVING THROUGH several long-overdue cultural reckonings. Highlighted in recent years are centuries of inequality for women, people of color, members of the LGBTQ community, the physically and developmentally disabled, and other marginalized groups. The impact and staying power of movements such as #MeToo and Black Lives Matter are evidence that millions are fed up and no longer satisfied with a status quo they believe is marked by systemic racism, sexual misconduct, and income inequality. Among their demands are equity, corporate diversity, and criminal justice reform.

Nowhere has this shift been more apparent than in the language we use every day. Changed forever are societal norms and expectations around how we treat and speak with one another. As an extension of this new normal, brands are working hard to communicate with this same understanding.

If your organization has less reason to be outspoken around these issues, so be it. If you believe some of these recommendations are more applicable than others, do what feels right. What is apparent to me is that brands that are truly in touch with their key stakeholders and that can more easily articulate their mission, values, and ideals will (a) be less likely to confront a reputational threat and (b) be better prepared to successfully navigate one when it does arise.

The recommendations and examples presented in this chapter aren't intended to sound self-righteous, judgmental, or as political statements; they're a summation of my personal observations of how brands have effectively communicated cultural competence (defined as the "ability to understand, appreciate and interact with people from cultures or belief systems different from one's own").[1] Consider these best practices for the new normal.

ADDRESSING A WATERSHED MOMENT

In the wake of George Floyd's murder by a Minneapolis police officer on May 25, 2020, as protests and demonstrations were taking place around the globe, employers had their eyes opened to how issues around racial injustice impacted their workplace, customers, and others in their ecosystem. It was too significant, too historic a moment to let pass without a thoughtful response and a commitment to be part of the solution. As a result, many of our clients felt compelled to take a variety of actions and to communicate about those actions.

For the remainder of 2020, we collaborated on letters, social media posts, and virtual town halls as C-suites brainstormed and talked about meaningful new initiatives. The messages echoed a similar theme: we commit to becoming a more informed and more outspoken organization when it comes to recognizing and calling out systemic racism and other injustices, big and small.

Some messages that voiced support for peaceful demonstrations taking place around the globe were well received. Others necessitated follow-up communications—and even apologies—if the initial statements were perceived as underwhelming, poorly worded, or only appearing to do the bare minimum. The media was paying close attention, and there were widespread accusations of virtue signaling. According to

The Atlantic, "American brands have rushed to show where they stand, but it's still uncertain what they intend to offer—what they can offer—beyond greater awareness of their existence and a vague sense of virtue."[2]

The New Morality of Doing Business

Although many, if not most, CEOs had been hesitant to speak out about social issues for fear of offending and alienating certain stakeholders, most now recognize that consumers' increased expectations are part of the new normal. No longer can our most recognizable and public-facing brands remain neutral on some of our most significant social issues.

Columnist David Von Drehle summed up this "new morality of doing business" in early 2022.

> *Gone are the days of the Friedman Doctrine, enunciated in 1970 by the influential laissez-faire economist Milton Friedman. The social responsibility of a corporation, Friedman declared, is exclusively to maximize the satisfaction of shareholders—measured by rising revenue and stock prices (unless the shareholders themselves decide otherwise). Executives are to think only of the bottom line . . . the doctrine remained in favor until the gap between flat wages and steeply escalating super-wealth grew so great that the folks in the penthouses began worrying about folks with pitchforks.[3]*

To the point made in *The Atlantic* article, how do brands back up their words to ensure they live these values every day? You can be certain that constituents will hold them accountable if they say the right thing in the moment, only to revert to a more conveniently neutral position.

The more a brand is recognized as socially conscious or outspokenly progressive, the stronger their position to be an industry leader on these issues. However, be forewarned: the more out-front a brand is on a topic, the greater the pressure and expectations there will be to practice what it preaches. It makes sense. Supporters of an altruistic brand are idealists on some level. As a result, they'll be even more prone to alienation if their favorite brand appears to merely pay lip service to its stated mission and ideals.

With our interconnected global economy, many brands are dependent on partners, suppliers, and subcontractors. They should be aware of how these groups are also viewed in light of *their* commitment to human rights and social justice.

The concept of *reputation by association*, addressed in the previous chapter, matters in the for-profit world as well. For instance, while Apple has a strong domestic reputation in the United States, it's still impacted by the behavior of subcontractors such as Foxconn, which makes iPhones. In 2010, eighteen Foxconn factory workers attempted suicide, and in 2019, an excessive number of temporary workers were reportedly found on the iPhone line at one of the factories, a violation of Chinese labor law.[4] Workers' rights activists and the press expected Apple to be accountable for these issues.

So how do brands appropriately communicate in an environment where best practices are rapidly evolving? After all, even the most well-intentioned among us can feel uncertain how to navigate this new normal. It's not enough to have one's heart in the right place; we must listen and learn from others and commit to doing the hard work of making change. Otherwise, communications at the core of these efforts could fall flat or, even worse, offend.

I've advised many clients through diversity, equity, and inclusion (DEI)–related issues and recognized some universal truths about these successful communications. Messages that stood above the rest typically included some combination of the following precepts.

Do Your Homework and Avoid Assumptions

Our upbringing profoundly influences the way we see the world and how we communicate. When people act differently or share an unfamiliar viewpoint, don't assume they're wrong or their opinion isn't valid. *Walk a mile in another's shoes* is the adage that applies here, as opposed to the golden rule. In short, people don't always want to be treated the same way *you* want to be treated; so make the effort to speak in a way that will resonate across a diverse set of stakeholders.

If drafting communications for a community other than your own, consider consulting members of that group, including activists and writers. This way, your words will ring authentic and true. For example, many well-meaning individuals do not realize that "homosexual" is considered a derogatory term. LGBTQ advocates ask of us, "Please use *gay* or *lesbian* to describe people attracted to members of the same sex. Because of the clinical history of the word 'homosexual,' it is aggressively used by anti-gay extremists to suggest that gay people are somehow diseased or psychologically/emotionally disordered."[5]

Avoid terms that suggest gender bias or superiority. For instance, instead of assuming someone goes by *boyfriend* or *husband*, you're better off using *spouse* or *partner*. Instead of *chairman*, use *chair* or *chairperson*. Familiarize yourself with the latest terminology around gender expression. From universities to nonprofits to large corporate law firms, identifying pronouns now regularly appear in the signature of emails (e.g., he/she/they), so take note. Always look for ways to offer dignity to another whenever possible.

Get Personal

The countless Black lives tragically lost due to systemic racism have remained a statistic for far too long. No more. In letters to staff, customers, and other stakeholders, CEOs of major corporations named these victims, including George Floyd, Ahmaud Arbery, and Breonna Taylor, putting a human face on senseless tragedies. Identifying each victim of a brutal injustice underscored the toll of such ignorance as well as the dignity and respect these individuals deserved at the end of their lives but, tragically, were denied.

Communications that were heavily criticized included those that used generic phrases such as "members of the Black community" and "people of color," or that drew comparisons between the societal impact of the COVID-19 pandemic and systemic racism, purposefully or

inadvertently. The moment called for a fresh perspective and a new way
of communicating: a more personal, empathetic, and intimate tone.

THE UNDERWHELMING RESPONSE

Boston University's president found himself in hot water for a letter sent in June 2020, in which he linked racial injustices and social activism unfolding around the globe to the campus being shut down due to COVID-19.

"Our commitment to restoring our residential campus," Robert Brown wrote, "is made all the more important by the divisions in our country."[6]

Hundreds of students complained that equating the two in any way was inappropriate and that Brown's message advocating for social justice was disproportionately mild. Two days later, Brown sent another letter, using less ambiguous language to condemn systemic racism.

> In my [first] letter, I spoke like the engineer I was trained to be, trying to look ahead to a time when our community can work together to push out racism and bigotry. . . . Today, this letter is from my heart, and my heart is with all of you who feel the dehumanizing sting of racism, and who lose a part of your own life every time a Black man or woman is murdered because they are Black.[7]

Clear and direct language was called for from the outset. If a leader isn't intrinsically wired to communicate appropriately in these moments, it's up to their advisers to counsel them on the proper messages.

Admit There's Work to Be Done

Some of the strongest corporate messages in the spring and summer of 2020 described DEI initiatives the organization was actively engaged in, while committing to others. Remember, this work is a continuous journey. Acknowledge where your brand might be falling short if sharing renewed efforts to meet specific benchmarks among this new set of expectations.

In 2020, the Associated Press reviewed the diversity reports from some major brands pledging solidarity with the Black community. It discovered "their efforts to recruit, maintain and promote minorities within their own ranks have fallen short."[8] Among the companies called out: Microsoft, Amazon, and Nike, all for having 10 percent or less of their executives, directors, or managers who were Black.[9] Nike's CEO John Donahoe wrote his employees that the company's "most important priority is to get our own house in order."[10]

Talk about Next Steps

Any communication articulating a brand's efforts to improve its internal culture should leave readers with a clear understanding of the next steps to be taken to achieve the stated goals. For example, brands committed to a more diverse workforce should articulate new recruiting and hiring practices as well as talent-development programs to support employees of color to ensure they receive the mentorship and support they need to advance in the organization. Just as important are follow-up communications to report on results over time.

In the spring of 2020, the athletic brand Adidas, which also owns Reebok, pledged to fill at least 30 percent of all new positions in the United States with Black and Latino people.[11] CEO Kasper Rørsted talked about the need to provide opportunities for employees of color that hadn't been as readily available to them as they had been for their White peers:

> *The events of the past two weeks have caused all of us to reflect on what we can do to confront the cultural and systemic forces that sustain racism. . . . We have had to look inward to ourselves as individuals and our organization and reflect on systems that disadvantage and silence Black individuals and communities.*[12]

Updates on the work of committees or groups tasked with diversity efforts should be shared across the organization, while candid feedback on their efforts should be encouraged.

To ensure a strong representation of multiple lived experiences and perspectives, consider employees at different levels and from across departments to take part in these initiatives. Make DEI resources available on your website or intranet so your workforce can stay apprised of progress made. This will prevent accusations that the process is closed off and not truly representative of the entire workforce.

Although a CEO will likely delegate a leader or different leaders to spearhead this important work, the chief executive should demonstrate their commitment by regularly communicating DEI priorities. Key is talking about them, not just as an additional piece of the brand's mission, but as inextricably linked.

LEADING FROM THE TOP

Tim Ryan started his new job as the US chair of PwC, also known as PricewaterhouseCoopers, one of the "Big Four" accounting firms, in July 2016. That same week, the separate fatal shootings by police officers of two Black men, Alton Sterling and Philando Castile, made national headlines. Days later, a sniper targeted and killed five White Dallas police officers.

It was an inflection point for Ryan, who's White and who oversees fifty thousand US employees. Despite the very real possibility that efforts to discuss what many considered a third-rail issue could backfire, Ryan initiated conversations about race throughout the company. As he later reported, "The day wasn't easy, but it wasn't a disaster, either. For many White professionals at PwC, it was eye-opening to hear what their Black peers faced in terms of discrimination and inequity."[13]

Ryan didn't stop there. He started the CEO Action for Diversity and Inclusion, described on its website as "the largest CEO-driven business commitment to drive measurable action and meaningful change in advancing diversity, equity and inclusion in the workplace."[14] As of this writing, more than two thousand CEOs and presidents have signed the pledge.

PwC's launching of the CEO Action commitment has burnished the company's already strong reputation. In fact, more than 70 percent of those polled in a 2016 study said they are more likely to view a company in a more positive way if it addresses race publicly.[15]

Articulate Ways to Give Back

Demonstrate advocacy with a meaningful contribution, either monetarily or through volunteer hours, to a nonprofit whose cause aligns with your brand's mission. In the aftermath of the social justice demonstrations of 2020, PwC agreed to give employees forty hours a year to devote to community service. Volunteer opportunities that open our eyes to the struggles of others can't help but make us more informed and empathetic citizens.

Pro bono work on behalf of a nonprofit is another effective way to live your brand's values. Depending on the product or service you deliver, think of the unique ways you can help. For instance, immigration attorneys might offer free legal services to refugees from abroad to help guide them on a path to US citizenship. Pro bono work will boost morale, provide growth opportunities for colleagues, and have an overall positive impact on your brand's overall reputation.

DEBRIEF

Whether you work in a corporate environment or one without a significant human resources framework, acting and speaking in a way that communicates understanding, sensitivity, and respect is crucial to reputation. Education and awareness around these issues is critical to being an effective communicator in the twenty-first century. Following the guidance I've offered is a good start:

- Do your homework and avoid assumptions.

- Get personal.

- Admit there's work to be done.

- Talk about next steps.

- Articulate ways to give back.

Just as brands engage outside legal and communications experts to help them navigate a series of unknowns, they should consider culture and workplace issues a specialty that requires the counsel of trained professionals. Bringing in an outside DEI expert sends a signal to employees, potential employees, and others that you prioritize these teachings and principles. An objective third party can be especially helpful when there might be differences of opinion on goal setting or on whether a company is implementing change fast enough.

The term *diversity* applies to gender, culture, religion, race, ethnicity, age, physical and cognitive challenges, sexual orientation, and socioeconomic status. Continue to solicit feedback on initiatives and communications from multiple perspectives to ensure you're taking action and speaking with a voice that's informed and in touch with your community as well as the culture writ large.

12

LESSONS FROM
A YEAR IN CRISIS

I BEGAN WRITING THIS BOOK in 2020, a year filled with one unprecedented issue and crisis after another: COVID-19, an awakening to widespread racial injustice, historic levels of unemployment, and election-related chaos. Many employers found themselves on their own when it came to providing guidance and setting policy during a rapidly evolving global pandemic, while others struggled with how to talk about these momentous events. Just as necessity is the mother of invention, communications and crisis response plans normally developed over weeks or months had to come together in just days or even hours.

According to PwC's *Global Crisis Survey 2021: Building Resilience for the Future*, "Only 35 percent of respondents had a crisis response plan that was 'very relevant' [for the pandemic], which means the majority didn't design their plans to be 'crisis agnostic'—a hallmark of a resilient organisation."[1]

The pandemic validated that crisis planning must account for a multitude of scenarios. It was also a reminder that the most important communication begins internally, within an organization. It forced businesses to not just consider the product they produce or the service they offer, but to also focus on their employees' well-being and the day-to-day operations many took for granted. Whether a lack of customers or supply chain issues directly impacted an organization, the pandemic was universal and touched all our lives.

NAVIGATING FROM CHAOS TO CONTROL

Our firm met with clients, virtually, as they made decision after decision about safety protocols and business continuity, calls that practically had to be communicated in real time. We worked with numerous leadership teams that were counted on to deliver uninterrupted services, including those in charge of healthcare organizations, apartment communities, and banks. It required an all-hands-on-deck effort during a year in which many of the fundamental principles of protecting and defending a brand's reputation capital rang true.

Remain Flexible

In February and early March 2020, employers were communicating about the need to have extra hand sanitizer available at the office and enhancing cleaning protocols after workers had left for the day. Then, on March 4, we received an email from a client, the owner and operator of several office buildings, notifying us that a tenant had an employee who recently returned to the United States from London and was feeling ill. While there was no certainty about his diagnosis, office leadership made the tough decision to have all employees work from home until his negative COVID status could be confirmed.

That weekend, I received several texts and emails from clients responding to our firm's earlier outreach about planning for the spread of coronavirus and the likely restrictions to be imposed as a result. They sensed conditions were worsening, COVID cases and deaths were escalating, and they wanted to discuss messaging first thing Monday morning.

Among those communications we drafted for clients during the week of March 9 were those announcing restrictions on domestic and foreign business travel, the closing of common spaces at residential communities such as gyms and business centers, and new protocols for doctor's office visits.

Uncertainty ruled and world markets were in free fall. The following week would see three of the largest percentage drops in the history of the Dow Jones Industrial Average. To illustrate just how quickly events on the ground were changing, much of the language in a crisis response plan we drafted on March 11 was obsolete by that evening. Messages for COVID-related scenarios had to be time-stamped, not just for the day they were updated but for the hour. That's the same day the National Basketball Association suspended its season, and Hollywood power couple Tom Hanks and Rita Wilson announced they had tested positive for the virus.

Soon, mayors across much of the country were implementing serious restrictions, including limiting indoor capacity on retail businesses and restaurants. In Boston, the Sunday before St. Patrick's Day, bars and taverns were forced to close except for takeout service. Despite the Federal Reserve cutting rates to zero to try to get ahead of Monday's opening bell, March 16 was the second-worst day in the history of the Dow Jones. COVID wasn't just a full-blown health crisis; it was a crisis for every brand that had to figure out how to function in a world where employees and customers were no longer allowed to congregate.

In early April, as the pandemic's stranglehold grew tighter, organizations scrambled to ensure they could serve those who depended on them—despite having to quickly close offices and facilities like warehouses and factories.

Businesses adapted by incorporating video calls, instant messaging tools, and other technology to facilitate communication and collaboration during remote work. Our firm supported clients as they established telemedicine, online learning, and other virtual services in extraordinarily short order. In addition, leaders worked to make sure employees understood their roles and expectations in working remotely full time.

During this time of great uncertainty, several principles of crisis communications were reinforced.

Stay Informed

At our own office, staff monitored news on the websites of the Centers for Disease Control and Prevention (CDC) and the World Health Organization (WHO) throughout the day to keep track of any alerts, updates, or new guidelines. This ensured we didn't recommend policies to our clients that were already outdated or obsolete. Guidance was multilayered and could often be confusing as state and federal orders at times contradicted the guidelines or orders implemented by individual municipalities.

Familiarity with the decisions made in other cities and states provided guidance and justification for our recommendations. We also considered how well-known and respected brands were responding or engaged in creative problem-solving. This additional context proved especially helpful and instructive.

Owners of large assets such as office buildings, or agencies in charge of transportation infrastructure, regularly stay on top of alerts from knowledgeable and credible sources such as the US State Department and Homeland Security, so they're aware of elevated threat levels and can respond accordingly.

The need to stay informed was readily apparent during the social justice demonstrations that filled city streets across America in 2020. While these events were mostly peaceful, the owners and operators of prominent downtown real estate kept close watch on the crowds and potential flare-ups of violence using real-time monitoring software. This software aggregated all sorts of data, including thousands of media reports and social media posts.

The properties, many of which include ground-floor retail, had those businesses boarded up and had extra security on hand in the event things got out of control. In addition, alternative entrances and exits had to be arranged so personnel working inside the buildings could safely travel to and from work.

Manage Expectations

In the early days of COVID-19, before working from home became the norm in many industries, employers were faced with what to do if one of their workers demonstrated symptoms of COVID-19 or just wasn't feeling well. Such predicaments included: "Should an employee come into the office if they had been overseas recently?" and "Should an employee be allowed to come into the office if their child might have been exposed to someone who tested positive?" Although it now seems like a no-brainer, instructing employees to go home and self-quarantine for several days felt, at the time, like extreme measures.

A vital function of early-stage communications when facing such uncertainty is managing expectations. In addition to sharing new office policies and recommendations around personal hygiene to prevent the spread of the virus, we worked with clients on the process of rapidly canceling scheduled appearances at industry conferences, conventions, and sales meetings. These mandates helped set the tone by taking the pressure off individual employees to make these decisions for themselves

We all need time to process information and adjust. Ensuring advance notice was especially critical when our firm worked side by side with one of Massachusetts' largest cities during the onset of COVID. For instance, many families needed a backup plan for child/elderly care and many of those whose loved ones relied on home healthcare workers had to come up with alternative arrangements. For this reason, it was essential that we provided ample notice of new ordinances—such as a curfew or stay-at-home order—and that we continued to remind those affected as the change went into effect.

We also had to over-communicate with partners such as the school district, first responders, and several different city departments prior to general announcements so they weren't caught flatfooted when they started getting questions about how they were impacted. We knew that if the superintendent of schools or the head of a local nonprofit received press calls and said they weren't consulted, it wouldn't be a good look for anyone.

Don't Allow a Messaging Vacuum

Be sure to give midlevel managers the information they need to speak confidently. While C-suite executives should be the first to communicate organization-wide, recognize those who can also be important emissaries. Make sure they're up to speed on the latest developments and won't be caught off guard with a question from the staff they weren't anticipating. Anyone authorized to share information about an issue should have access to the same messaging as their colleagues. Ensure no one is using yesterday's messages when today's may be totally different.

Solicit feedback from those outside the crisis response team to ensure you're not operating in a bubble. Ask managers to let you know what questions and concerns they're hearing, both internally and externally, so you'll know what needs to be addressed and added to future communications.

Make Your Case

If accused of something you *did* do, but with good reason, take the time to explain your rationale. As I've shared, never assume that every occasion for which you face criticism deserves an apology. For instance, independent schools saw a sharp decrease in revenue during the spring and summer of 2020. Rather than lay off staff, many schools opted to apply for federal dollars through the Small Business Administration's Paycheck Protection Program (PPP).

Sensing that the optics of these elite private institutions applying for government funds might not go over well with the public, heads of school planned for the potential blowback. Their vigilance was justified. Leading newspapers, including the *Washington Post* and the *New York Times*, ran stories on prestigious schools nationwide that applied for and received PPP funds.

Although some schools were shamed into returning the federal funds, others stood firm. They explained that, even after significant belt-tightening and endowment withdrawals, the uncertainty of being able to hold on to key staff remained. This was because most school costs are fixed, with more than half of operating budgets committed to salaries, benefits, and financial aid. The dip in revenue was the result of everything from decreased philanthropy to an increased need for student financial aid.

In Uncertain Times, Overcommunicate

In the early days of COVID, it seemed as if every brand involved in our lives, from automobile manufacturers to credit card companies, was blasting out mass emails. Businesses explained what they were doing to ensure uninterrupted service, how they were allowing for late payments, or how they were protecting their workforce from the virus. While some news coverage at the time was highly critical of these communications, characterizing them as unnecessary, I'd beg to differ.

We all perceive messages differently. Once COVID-19 hit, some could only accept guidance based on where they were personally in adapting to the new pandemic reality. Message consistency and the frequency with which organizations communicated served as small signs of stability during an uncertain and frightening time. It's better to be accused of overcommunicating during a crisis than undercommunicating.

At the same time, every email doesn't need to be long and in-depth. Stay focused on high-level messages and need-to-know information. When things become chaotic, don't overwhelm recipients with unnecessary details. Yes, anticipate potential follow-up questions and provide additional resources, but don't write 1,000 words when 250 will do. You can always hyperlink to webpages or microsites with more specific information for those who want it.

Early in the pandemic, I believed that the steady stream of communications that normally would've been considered overkill, was welcome. During episodes of unease, confusion, and concern, we turn to our leaders to guide and reassure us that everything will turn out OK. An important piece of this is providing clearly written communications that contain relevant, timely, and actionable information. In a crisis, it's a lack of communication that will sow confusion.

Never . . . Stop . . . Planning

At the onset of COVID-19, the situation evolved rapidly, and marketing and communications professionals triaged several scenarios for which communications were urgently required. Part of navigating a crisis is also anticipating what's next by planning for the "what if?" At some point, response must pivot to proactive planning.

Even before governors issued stay-at-home orders throughout their states, we engaged clients in conversations around exactly what they'd need if that did, in fact, occur. The key is to always stay one step ahead of developments to the extent that's possible. Construct a guide like the matrix of "if-then" scenarios featured in chapter 5, and think through all possible scenarios and outcomes and what communications would be necessary as a result of each one. It's considerably easier to convene leaders to make hard operational decisions and draft communications when they're not dealing with the additional stress than after those developments have already occurred.

DEBRIEF

There's nothing like a significant crisis to remind organizations which best practices they should follow to protect and defend their reputation. So consider just how valuable these lessons are from an entire year in crisis:

- Remain flexible.

- Stay informed.

- Manage expectations.

- Don't allow a messaging vacuum.

- In uncertain times, overcommunicate.

- Never . . . stop . . . planning.

While some crisis engagements are short-term, major emergencies such as responding to a pandemic, a natural gas explosion, or a bridge collapse can persist for weeks or even months.

During such unprecedented moments, your trusted crisis communications plan and training will be a foundation on which to build a robust response. So, when the time comes, turn to the best practices offered in these chapters. They are universal truths that can help steer you and your organization through even the most uncertain of times.

REPUTATION CAPITAL
CASE STUDIES

NOW THAT WE'VE TAKEN a deep dive into what and what *not* to do when it comes to building, protecting, and defending a reputation, let's take a closer look at two of the most well-known brand crises in recent years.

You'll recognize many of the recommendations as well as the pitfalls discussed in previous chapters, such as:

- blaming others for your crisis

- offering two different explanations for the same crisis

- letting the legal strategy overpower the PR strategy

In each example, good and bad decisions and communications are intertwined. In a crisis, perception can quickly become reality. For instance, it's possible that United Airlines regretted what happened as soon as their passenger was badly mistreated. Yet, because they *communicated* as if they didn't care, that was the narrative that took hold.

Each brand started out with ample reputation capital. But these offenses, both of which were triggered by customer-facing staff, were egregious enough that the initial communications set the tone for the entire response.

The case studies offer a turn-by-turn analysis of real-life crises so that you, the reader, can more easily recognize and understand how brands respond to a complex issue effectively and how they can avoid making the myriad of mistakes that so many often do.

A FAILURE TO ACCOMMODATE AND COMMUNICATE

UNITED AIRLINES' REPUTATION CAPITAL

United Airlines is the third-largest airline in the world, serving hundreds of destinations. On March 9, 2017, a story appeared in the leading public relations trade outlet *PR Week*, naming Oscar Munoz, the airlines' CEO, as its "Communicator of the Year." He was hailed for being a leader who "understands the value of communications" and who had personally "transformed the fortunes of the beleaguered airline, galvanized staff, and set the business on a smoother course."[1] All this, despite having to take two months off to undergo a heart transplant just six weeks after being named CEO.[2]

The honor made what occurred one month later all the more shocking: a crisis response that would memorialize Munoz's central role in a cautionary tale of how *not* to communicate when facing a severe reputational threat. The fact he had recently earned the *PR Week* recognition underscores the stark difference between proactive, positive public relations when times are good and an effective crisis response when a brand is at the center of a reputational firestorm.

The Crisis Event

It's 5:40 p.m. Central time on Sunday, April 9, 2017, when 69-year-old Dr. David Dao Duy Anh, a Vietnamese American physician, boards United Express Flight 3411 at O'Hare International Airport in Chicago and takes his seat on board the Embraer 170 bound for Louisville, Kentucky.[3] With seventy passengers settling in on the full flight, four additional United crew members approach the gate and tell agents they must get to Louisville, where a plane on the ground needs a flight crew.

After unsuccessful offers of vouchers and seats on a flight the next day to entice passengers to give up their seats for the crew, a computer selects four passengers who will have to get off the plane. When Dr. Dao is informed that he's one of the four, he protests, insisting he needs to return to Louisville immediately to see a patient first thing the next morning. Unable to convince Dr. Dao, the flight crew summons the Chicago Department of Aviation Security. Three officers board the aircraft, forcibly remove him from his seat, and drag him screaming down the aisle.

According to the *New York Times*, Dao "screamed as a security officer wrestled him out of his seat and dragged him down the aisle by his arms. His glasses slid down his face, and his shirt rose above his midriff as uniformed officers followed."[4] Dao's attorney reports his client suffered a concussion, a broken nose, injury to the sinuses, and the loss of two front teeth during the melee.[5] As if the optics couldn't get any worse, Dao's fellow passengers are seen and heard on smartphone video, screaming in outrage at his treatment and pleading with the officers and flight crew for it to stop.

The *Washington Post* reports that the first passenger videos of the incident appear on Twitter at 7:30 p.m. EST on Sunday. One video will end up being viewed more than nineteen million times on Facebook before it's no longer publicly available on the platform.[6]

Regardless of how it responds, United has a major crisis on its hands. Failing to de-escalate the situation, the flight crew forced a physical confrontation between law enforcement and a paying passenger when the health and safety of those on board the flight are clearly not at risk. The eyewitness videos alone are enough to keep the story in the headlines for days. But a series of mistakes by United's management makes matters worse. Here's a breakdown of what happens, along with my analysis:

Sunday evening, April 9

The airline issues its first official statement about the incident to the Louisville *Courier-Journal*:

Flight 3411 from Chicago to Louisville was overbooked. After our team looked for volunteers, one customer refused to leave the aircraft voluntarily and law enforcement was asked to come to the gate. We apologize for the overbook situation. Further details on the removed customer should be directed to authorities."[7]

ANALYSIS

Missteps

Being tone-deaf. It's clear United thought apologizing for overbooking the flight was a viable explanation for what occurred. "Flight 3411 from Chicago to Louisville was overbooked" might have been appropriate language had the airline been explaining why one of their flights arrived two hours late, but not in response to security dragging a bloodied passenger off a plane. The tone was condescending and not the least bit remorseful.

Victim shaming. The following line stated, "After our team looked for volunteers, one customer refused to leave the aircraft voluntarily and law enforcement was asked to come to the gate." This language suggested the passenger's behavior was so egregious that the only appropriate response was to call law enforcement. Yet overbookings occur every day in the airline industry. Once Dr. Dao was physically assaulted, the issue of the flight being overbooked or not became moot; there was simply no rationale for forcing a physical confrontation with a passenger who didn't pose a threat to anyone.

Avoiding accountability. The final line, "Further details on the removed customer should be directed to authorities" is language typically used in response to a crisis that's strictly a law-enforcement issue. That was not the case with Dr. Dao, not even close. There was no way United could ever shirk responsibility after what occurred. Social media users and the press would make sure of that.

When a company is still gathering all the facts, it can use the first public statement to buy time and act as a bridge to a more substantial response. While far from comprehensive, a more satisfactory communication from United at this time would've been:

A video on social media, which appears to depict the horrific treatment of a passenger on board a United flight, is disturbing and upsetting. We are working on gathering as much information as possible and will have more to say as soon as we do. The safety and well-being of our passengers is always our top priority.

Would that statement have explained what happened? No. Would it have provided any justification for the treatment of Dr. Dao? No. There's no justification for such treatment, other than if Dr. Dao had been actively threatening the safety of the flight and his fellow passengers.

What United needed to address first and foremost was what went through the heads of anyone watching the video (i.e., "How could any airline allow a passenger to be treated so cruelly?").

Monday morning, April 10

Outrage escalates on social media. Posters flood United's channels with angry comments and memes and demand to know what happened. United responds to these tweets with pieces of their statement from the night before. Once again, these communications are so tone-deaf, they appear to be responding to an alternative reality.

After noon, Oscar Munoz releases a second statement:

This is an upsetting event to all of us here at United. I apologize for having to re-accommodate these customers. Our team is moving with a sense of urgency to work with the authorities and conduct our own detailed review of what happened. We are also reaching out to this passenger to talk directly to him and further address and resolve this situation.[8]

ANALYSIS

Missteps

Using legalese. Use of the term *re-accommodate* was perceived by many as callous, overly technical, and indifferent. *Accommodate* is defined as "to provide with something desired, needed, or suited."[9] Try to reconcile that term with how security personnel wrestled Dr. Dao out of his seat and dragged him down the aisle. Once again, the disconnect was glaring. *Vanity Fair* called this "a tone-deafness that will go down in corporate PR history."[10]

While avoiding additional legal exposure must be a priority, the potential PR ramifications can be equally or even more significant. The issue was not Dr. Dao refusing to get off a flight. It was United allowing one of their passengers to be treated in such a way. Yet, in the drafting of this statement, it appeared legal considerations trumped PR.

The poorly worded apology compounded the damage and guaranteed a whole new round of media coverage. Hundreds of sarcastic memes appeared on social media mocking the statement. Some likened *re-accommodate*, the term United used to characterize the assault, to violent collisions on a football field; created parody ads ("If we cannot beat our competitors, we beat our customers!"); and made satirical pop culture references featuring *Fight Club* and *The Walking Dead*.

Avoiding accountability. While United was smart to point out that "our team is moving with a sense of urgency to work with the authorities and conduct our own detailed review of what happened," it neglected to say (a) whether those findings would be made public and (b) what potential action United would take as a result.

By 2017, it was no longer sufficient for a brand to say an investigation or review would take place. Long past was the time when supporters had blind trust in a brand to do the right thing. Today's consumers demand a level of corporate transparency and accountability commensurate with the severity of the transgression.

Lacking empathy. "This is an upsetting event to all of us here at United" might not have been victim shaming, but it did appear to be prioritizing the feelings of those at the airline over their brutally assaulted passenger. Typically, the public's reaction to such a claim is, "Who cares what those at United Airlines are feeling?"

Using impersonal terms. First, the statement tried to avoid singling out Dr. Dao by referring only to "these customers," as if all four of the passengers asked to give up their seats received identical treatment. Then, with this language, United only referred to "this passenger" when referencing him specifically. There are times when a generic description of a victim won't suffice, and this was one of them.

Monday evening, April 10

Compounding public outrage over the statement, an internal letter Munoz sent to United employees earlier in the day becomes public. Among the claims in the communication, the CEO asserts, "Our employees followed established procedures."

The letter went on to share details around the incident, saying Dao was "politely asked to deplane" and that "each time he refused and became more and more disruptive and belligerent."[11]

ANALYSIS

Missteps

Being inconsistent. Seemingly, neither Munoz nor his advisers took the time to think through how an internal letter could easily be shared with a reporter or via social media.

With the public now having access to both the employee letter and the public statements, Munoz appeared to be speaking out of both sides of his mouth, merely telling each stakeholder group what he thought they wanted to hear. The statement given to the media, already roundly criticized, sounded even more disingenuous. Although sending an entirely different message to employees than to the press may have once been feasible, it no longer is. The same information must be shared across all audiences.

Victim shaming, again. The employee letter doubled down on the airline's initial defense that "one customer refused to leave the aircraft voluntarily." Only this time, Dr. Dao was labeled "disruptive and belligerent."[12] The lack of empathy was, again, stunning.

No matter how inappropriately a customer is acting, that behavior will quickly be disregarded or forgotten if your brand's response is perceived as even worse than the actual event. That's especially true for airlines, which we expect to care for the safety and well-being of passengers from the time they board to the time they deplane.

With both messages under heavy criticism, members of Congress begin to weigh in, demanding investigations into the incident on board Flight 3411.

Tuesday, April 11

Less than 48 hours after security dragged Dr. Dao from his seat, the economic impact of the event and United's response hits the airline like a ton of bricks. Tuesday morning, the airline's stock plummets, with the shares of the airline down 6 percent and over a billion dollars in value.[13] Perhaps it's no coincidence that, later in the day, Munoz finally releases a statement effectively addressing the issue:

> *The truly horrific event that occurred on this flight has elicited many responses from all of us: outrage, anger, disappointment. I share all of those sentiments, and one above all: my deepest apologies for what happened. Like you, I continue to be disturbed by what happened on this flight and I deeply apologize to the customer forcibly removed and to all the customers aboard. No one should ever be mistreated this way.*
>
> *I want you to know that we take full responsibility, and we will work to make it right.*
>
> *It's never too late to do the right thing. I have committed to our customers and our employees that we are going to fix what's broken so this never happens again. This will include a thorough review of crew movement, our policies for incentivizing volunteers in these situations, how we handle oversold situations and an examination of how we partner with airport authorities and local law enforcement. We'll communicate the results of our review by April 30th.*
>
> *I promise you we will do better.*[14]

ANALYSIS

What United Got Right

Using the right description. United had previously described the incident as the "overbook situation" and then "upsetting." Now more accurate characterizations are assigned to the incident, such as "truly horrific." The guttural reaction to the video of Dr. Dao was, at last, being articulated appropriately by the responsible party.

Showing empathy. Finally thinking like a Flight 3411 passenger, or the millions who viewed the video online, Munoz described the range of emotions expressed, including outrage, anger, disappointment. The public had been making their feelings known since Sunday night. It should never have taken Munoz or his advisers so long to acknowledge this. United's first instinct, like so many brands in crisis, was to circle the wagons, act and speak defensively, and adopt an us-versus-them mentality.

Munoz's leaked internal message just a day earlier had doubled down on his support of the flight crew. In Tuesday's statement, Munoz announced, "crew movement" and "how we handle oversold situations" would be among those protocols and actions that would undergo a "thorough review." No longer could Munoz pretend that the conduct of flight personnel during the situation was beyond reproach.

Issuing a direct apology. Previously, Munoz had only apologized for overbooking a flight and having to "re-accommodate passengers." Now he "deeply apologize(d)" to Dr. Dao directly, something he should have articulated at least 24 hours earlier once the facts of what had occurred were clear. As we'll see in the next case study, a quick and heartfelt apology can go a long way toward remedying a situation and protecting a brand's reputation.

Being accountable. Until now, United resisted making a direct apology or stating, "We take full responsibility." While I wasn't privy to internal conversations, the company most likely wanted to avoid even greater legal exposure. In addition to taking responsibility, Munoz promised he would follow up within weeks with the results of an internal investigation.

Admitting their mistake. First, Munoz signaled that United's previous communications had fallen short, saying, "It's never too late to do the right thing." Recall that his internal letter had stated, "employees followed established procedures." Now he expressed a dramatically different sentiment: "I have committed to our customers and our employees that we are going to fix what's broken so this never happens again."

Anyone can hide behind policies or blame a crisis on the poor decisions of a single employee. To Munoz's credit, he acknowledged the buck stopped with him. The situation called for a close review of existing policies and a recognition that United either didn't enforce them properly or hadn't addressed certain vulnerabilities.

Wednesday, April 12

Munoz makes a bold but necessary move, sitting down for a taped television interview with *Good Morning America*. It pays off. The interview reveals a soft-spoken, apologetic, and sincere CEO, in direct contrast to the same chief executive who sounded tone-deaf and unremorseful in initial public statements.

Although issuing carefully vetted language is typically effective, it's harder to gauge the level of sincerity in a written statement than in a face-to-face interview. If a written statement in response to a crisis only escalates the situation, a brand must pivot and diverge from the safe route. Answering direct questions in person with straight answers communicates that a brand has nothing to hide.

Munoz arrived at *GMA* prepared, likely media trained, and ready with his key messages and an apology for all that had gone wrong over the previous sixty or so hours.

ANALYSIS

What United Got Right

Showing empathy. Munoz recognized this was an emotional issue for many, not one that required a long, drawn-out explanation. When asked what he thought when he first saw the video of Dr. Dao, the CEO's response included, "It's not so much what I thought, as what I felt. *Probably* the word shame came to mind."[15]

Getting a CEO to admit shame shouldn't be taken lightly, and yet it was totally appropriate in this case. There was no way to rationalize how Dr. Dao had been treated, and no technical explanation could or would ever bail Munoz or United out of the self-inflicted crisis. So the CEO finally reacted the way everyone else had reacted when they saw the video.

Naming the victim. For the first time, Munoz named the injured passenger, humanizing the face of suffering that millions had witnessed on video. "I apologize to Dr. Dao, his family, the passengers, our customers, our employees," he said to the correspondent.[16] The CEO acknowledging and expressing regret for how United handled the situation was crucial to restoring its reputation as an appealing choice for both air travelers and its employees.

Admitting their mistake. Some leaders don't just adapt during a crisis; they come around 180 degrees from where they first started. When pressed why his previous statements, both internally and externally, had been so lacking, Munoz conceded, "My initial words fell short of truly expressing what we were feeling. And that's something I've learned from. The expression of apology . . . is an important part of a conversation like this."[17]

Outrage expressed on social media is often the result of a mob mentality and doesn't always accurately reflect the general public's feelings. The sentiment surrounding United's response, however, was unanimous. Although consumers can forgive bad brand behavior, an inability to learn from one's own mistakes is often viewed as inexcusable.

Being accountable. When asked what went wrong, Munoz didn't blame the crew. Instead, he took responsibility, stating, "It was a system failure," and explained he had not given the crew the tools they needed to address the situation effectively. Perhaps, most critically, when asked if Dr. Dao was at fault in any way, Munoz signaled he genuinely understood what was at stake. "No," he responded, after hesitating slightly, "he can't be . . . no one should be treated that way, period."[18]

DEBRIEF

In the weeks that followed, a sampling of United's public statements reflected its growth during the ordeal:

> *This horrible situation has provided a harsh learning experience from which we will take immediate, concrete action.*
>
> *We will fully review and improve our training programs to ensure our employees are prepared and empowered to put our customers first. Our values—not just systems—will guide everything we do.*[19]

Making good on sharing the results of its internal investigation, United, at the end of April, announced "10 substantial changes to how it flies, serves and respects its customers," including:

- limiting the use of law enforcement to safety and security issues only

- not requiring customers already seated on the plane to give up their seat involuntarily

- reducing the amount of overbooking[20]

The press release included key words like *respect, dignity, profound,* and *meaningful,* some of which appeared more than once. For example, *customer* appeared eleven times, including in a quote from Munoz stating, "Our customers should be at the center of everything we do, and these changes are just the beginning of how we will earn back their trust."

When Dr. Dao's lawyers announced a financial settlement with the airline, they praised the embattled CEO:

> *Mr. Munoz said he was going to do the right thing, and he has. In addition, United has taken full responsibility for what happened on Flight 3411, without attempting to blame others. . . . For this acceptance of corporate accountability, United is to be applauded.*[21]

Approximately three weeks after the incident on board Flight 3411, United and three of its competitors testified on Capitol Hill. "This is a turning point for United," Munoz pledged. "In that moment, for our customers and our company, we failed, and so as CEO, at the end of the day, that is on me."[22]

When all was said and done, the Transportation Department didn't fine United. Officials explained to the *Washington Post*, "Investigators found no evidence of race or nationality-based discrimination in the incident."[23] United's share price rebounded as its crisis response improved. In fact, by late 2018, shares hit a record high.

One Year Later

In March 2018, a French bulldog puppy suffocated during a United flight from Houston to New York. According to the puppy's owner, who was traveling with her two children, a flight attendant instructed her to place the family pet in its carrier in the overhead compartment for the flight. When the plane landed in New York, the puppy was no longer breathing.[24]

This time, United's statement sounded genuinely remorseful for what had taken place:

> *This was a tragic accident that should have never occurred. We accept full responsibility for this tragedy and express our deepest condolences to the family and are committed to supporting them. We are thoroughly investigating what occurred to prevent this from ever happening again.*[25]

The airline didn't escape criticism, but it did accept responsibility for what occurred and acknowledged that the flight attendant had acted improperly. United had learned that you can't hide behind rules and regulations or stiff legal language, especially in a crisis sparked by an emotional passenger event.

AN EXTRA HOT CUP OF HUMILITY

STARBUCKS' REPUTATION CAPITAL

From the time Starbucks was founded in 1971, opening in Seattle's Pike Place Market, it built a reputation as an employee-friendly business. Not long after Howard Schultz became CEO in 1987, the brand earned its progressive bona fides by offering "full health benefits to eligible full- and part-time employees, including coverage for domestic partnerships."[26] In addition, Starbucks embraced initiatives focused on issues such as diversity, competitive wages, and ethical coffee-sourcing standards.[27]

When Kevin Johnson succeeded Schultz as CEO in 2017, he made it clear that the coffee chain, with more than thirty-one thousand stores worldwide, would lean into its well-established values. "Will I continue on the social impact agenda as it relates to the core values of the company? Absolutely," Johnson told *Business Insider*. The story went on to report that "Starbucks' decision to take action on certain social issues doesn't just make for progressive feel-good stories," Johnson said. "It's also a strategic way to attract and retain engaged employees who feel connected to the coffee chain."[28]

The Crisis Event

On Thursday, April 12, 2018, police respond to a call from the store manager at a Philadelphia Starbucks, who reported feeling threatened by two men. The recording of the call to 911 would later reveal her saying, "I have two gentlemen at my cafe that are refusing to make a purchase or leave."[29] As the two African American men, Donte Robinson and Rashon Nelson, are arrested, a bystander records the episode on a smartphone. Once posted to Twitter, the video goes viral. The incident spurs the creation of the hashtag *#BoycottStarbucks*. Customers and the general public demand a response and an explanation.

Saturday, April 14

As the facts trickle out, it's revealed that Robinson and Nelson had merely been waiting for a business associate to arrive for a meeting. The Philadelphia Police Department and the mayor's office quickly launch separate investigations to determine whether the incident was the result of racial bias.

Philadelphia Mayor Jim Kenney releases a statement saying the incident "appears to exemplify what racial discrimination looks like in 2018." According to the *Philadelphia Inquirer*, the city's police commissioner, Richard Ross, posts on Facebook that the "officers did not do anything wrong."[30]

Even with some different interpretations of what occurred, the facts are clear enough that Starbucks takes to social media.

> *We apologize to the two individuals and our customers and are disappointed this led to an arrest. We take these matters seriously and clearly have more work to do when it comes to how we handle incidents in our stores. We are reviewing our policies and will continue to engage with the community and the police department to try to ensure these types of situations never happen in any of our stores.*[31]

ANALYSIS

What Starbucks Got Right

Apologizing. When facing a crisis and fearing legal exposure, too many brands have difficulty saying, "We're sorry." While this first public statement could have been more robust, Starbucks deserved credit for starting with an apology. It immediately communicated remorse for what occurred.

Missteps

Missing the point. The apology was so generic that it didn't differentiate between the two men and other Starbucks' customers. Most glaringly, it didn't mention race at all. Considering Starbucks' substantial reputation capital around issues of diversity and equity, the statement felt underwhelming and lackluster.

Responding too slowly. Two whole days passed since the video of the arrests was first posted before Starbucks released this statement. Management may have been waiting to confirm all the facts of what had occurred, but there's always something that can be said in the interim. For example, 24 hours earlier, they could have issued a statement such as:

> *We are aware of the video on social media, which appears to show two men being arrested on Thursday at one of our locations in Philadelphia. We are currently engaged in conversations with eyewitnesses, including law enforcement, as we await the findings of the city's investigations. Starbucks is committed to creating a culture of belonging, where everyone is welcome and treated with dignity and respect. We will have more to say once we have a clearer understanding of what occurred.*

Late Saturday, after its statement is criticized, Starbucks posts a letter from CEO Johnson on its website. It includes these passages:

> *First, to once again express our deepest apologies to the two men who were arrested with a goal of doing whatever we can to make things right. Second, to let you know of our plans to investigate the pertinent facts and make any necessary changes to our practices that would help prevent such an occurrence from ever happening again. And third, to reassure you that Starbucks stands firmly against discrimination or racial profiling. . . .*
>
> *I hope to meet personally with the two men who were arrested to offer a face-to-face apology. . . . We have immediately begun a thorough investigation of our practices. In addition to our own review, we will work with outside experts and community leaders to understand and adopt best practices. The video shot by customers*

is very hard to watch and the actions in it are not representative of our Starbucks Mission and Values. . . .

Finally, to our partners who proudly wear the green apron and to customers who come to us for a sense of community every day: You can and should expect more from us. We will learn from this and be better.[32]

ANALYSIS

What Starbucks Got Right

Apologizing. CEO Johnson began the letter reiterating the mea culpa expressed in the social post. He expressed his wish to apologize to the two men face-to-face, then communicated to those working in Starbucks stores worldwide that they should expect more from their leadership.

Accepting responsibility. Johnson didn't try to stick up for corporate policies. Rather, he conceded that those policies had failed and needed to be improved. Unlike United Airlines, whose response was critiqued in the previous case study, Starbucks didn't give a rote statement that the manager had just followed company policy. Instead, the brand acknowledged its policies had proven inadequate.

Empathizing. Unlike the United Airlines response, it was obvious that Johnson had watched the actual video. He stated, "The video shot by customers is very hard to watch and the actions in it are not representative of our Starbucks Mission and Values."

Being proactive. Johnson used each paragraph to share what steps Starbucks was taking to learn from the incident and prevent it from happening again. These steps included launching an internal investigation and meeting with customers, community members, and lawmakers in Philadelphia, in addition to providing additional training for employees.

Using the right language. Unlike United Airlines, Starbucks didn't use legalese such as "re-accommodate" in this letter. It was clear, straightforward, and used the appropriate descriptors. The letter began referencing the incident as "reprehensible," which is exactly what it was. From the get-go, readers knew the company wasn't tak-ing the incident lightly.

Missteps

Making excuses. The only reference to the employee at the center of this crisis was, "Our store manager never intended for these men to be arrested and this should never have escalated as it did." But the facts are that she did call the police, it did escalate, and the men were arrested.

Although it's admirable that Johnson didn't throw the employee under the bus, to suggest the manager had no inclination of what might occur when she dialed 911 felt rather tone-deaf. It was as if Starbucks was so focused on the larger injustice of potential discrim-ination that it wasn't acknowledging the poor decision-making that had led to the actual incident.

Sunday, April 15

A prominent Philadelphia activist leads a protest at the Starbucks loca-tion, demanding that the manager who dialed 911 be terminated. About seventy-five individuals show up for the noon protest.[33]

A video of Johnson is posted on Starbucks' website and shared on social media. Toward the end of the message, the CEO acknowledges, "Now, there have been some calls for us to take action [against] the store manager. I believe that blame is misplaced. In fact, I think the focus of fixing this—I own it. This is a management issue. And I am accountable."

ANALYSIS

What Starbucks Got Right

Providing visual content. Johnson demonstrated his excellent communication skills by staring straight into the camera and saying exactly what stakeholders wanted to hear. While statements or an over-the-phone interview with a reporter are acceptable for news-paper and online reporting, video and audio lend themselves to television and radio for obvious reasons, increasing the chances that content will be included in coverage.

Being responsive. After approximately 24 hours of feedback from the initial statement and letter, Johnson acknowledged some of the online chatter by addressing the status of the store manager. This was a perfect example of what it means to have a crisis strategy that reflects the realities on the ground: listening to criticism, then considering what key messages to adapt so that any subsequent statements are as spot-on as possible.

Starbucks had complete control over the content of the video, so it would have been easy enough for Johnson to avoid talking about the manager who called 911. Instead, he realized critics would have quickly pointed this out, so he addressed the issue head-on.

Missteps
None.

Starbucks decides the store manager who accused the two men of loitering won't face discipline. While Johnson does a solid job of articulating why ("This is a management issue"), protests erupt outside the Philadelphia store in the following days. The crowd voices its displeasure, perceiving the unwillingness to discipline as a lack of accountability.

Monday, April 16

Protests resume at the Starbucks, where about forty demonstrators, including a city councilwoman, fill the cafe.[34] That morning, Johnson goes on *Good Morning America* for a live interview. During his appearance, he powerfully communicates his key messages:

- The outcome was reprehensible.

- I personally apologize to the two gentlemen.

- It's my responsibility to ensure we fix it.

Johnson acknowledges that it was inappropriate to engage the police, and, "What happened to those two gentlemen was wrong." But when asked if the store manager would face any disciplinary action, he, again, holds firm: "While I know it's easy for me to say and point blame to one person in this incident, my responsibility is to look not only to that individual, but look more broadly at the circumstances that set that up just to ensure that this never happens again."[35]

In his final answer, Johnson says that if he were able to sit down and have a dialogue with the two men who were arrested, he would "invite them to join me in finding a constructive way to solve this issue."

ANALYSIS

What Starbucks Got Right

Everything. The post-interview chitchat between Robyn Roberts and co-anchor George Stephanopoulos said it all:

> **Stephanopoulos:** *That was really something. You know, we have seen a lot of corporate officials, a lot of public leaders, in trouble and have to apologize. This guy did not hedge, took full responsibility, said he's going to fix it. No equivocation. Textbook.*

> **Roberts:** *I know. We rarely see that from a CEO. He wasn't mincing words at all.*

Missteps

None. Not long after the interview, it was reported that the two men who were arrested agreed to meet with Johnson.

Just as its leadership demonstrates how to respond to one crisis effectively, Starbucks is blindsided by another. Late Monday, three-month-old video surfaces in which a dark-skinned male is denied entry to a Starbucks restroom right after a light-skinned male is allowed access in the same Southern California location. The brand now faces two very public incidents of alleged racial discrimination.

Starbucks posts the following statement:

Please know that we take this video and the commentary around it very seriously and are working closely with the team to learn from our mistakes. As you may have read in the letter from our CEO, we are fully investigating our store practices and guidelines across the company. In addition to our own review we will work with outside experts and community leaders to understand and adopt best practices, including unconscious bias training.[36]

Tuesday, April 17

In a new video, Johnson announces, as a first step, that all eight thousand US Starbucks stores will close on May 29 for a half day of racial bias training. The training will be provided to nearly 175,000 partners (employees) across the country and will become part of the onboarding process for new hires. Johnson notes that nationally recognized DEI experts will design the curriculum, and he pledges to make the training materials available for other companies to use.[37]

ANALYSIS

What Starbucks Got Right

Being transparent. Providing an update on the situation in Philadelphia, Johnson reports that he met with the two men who were arrested. He describes how he apologized and says they had "a very emotional and a very constructive conversation." He talked about what he'd been doing with his time in Philadelphia, including meetings with the mayor, the police commissioner, community leaders, and Starbucks employees.

Laying out the next steps. Johnson announced the May 29 trainings, a bold corporate initiative for sure. He described the purpose as "to listen and learn" and "craft a path forward" so that "every single customer that walks in our door feels welcome and safe."

Bringing in the experts. Lending the trainings instant credibility, the curriculum would be developed in partnership with nationally recognized experts in confronting racial bias, including the NAACP and the Anti-Defamation League. Partnering with recognized third-party experts in an area of perceived vulnerability communicates that a brand isn't just looking to respond to an issue but to become a true thought leader committed to ensuring best practices.

Paying it forward. Because Starbucks was committed to developing best-in-class training and had the resources to do so, it was a no-brainer to make those materials available to other businesses. Yet not every brand would've thought to do so. It was a wise move on Starbucks' part and completely in line with the progressive values and inclusive work environment they'd fostered over decades.

Missteps

None.

Wednesday, April 18

Starbucks founder Howard Schultz, then chairman, makes his first broadcast appearance since the Philadelphia arrest on *CBS This Morning*. The interview is conducted across a table at a Starbucks. This sends a message that the company's leadership "gets it" and aren't sequestered in some tall office building, out of touch with what their employees and customers are seeing and hearing in their cafes every day.

Like Johnson, the chairman talks about how the brand is committed to making amends and says that the planned training is "just the first step." Speaking with CBS's Gayle King, he confirms that the store manager left the company. He also announces that Starbucks would look to partner with Donte Robinson and Rashon Nelson, perhaps in the real estate venture they were meeting at the Philadelphia Starbucks to discuss at the time they were arrested.

ANALYSIS

What Starbucks Got Right

Being consistent. We heard the words Schultz used to describe the incident: embarrassed, ashamed, and, of course, reprehensible. Uniform messaging ensures that if someone read only one statement from Starbucks or saw only one video or interview with its leadership, there would be no mistaking how the company had responded and how seriously they took the incident.

Demonstrating competence. When asked, Schultz defined unconscious bias, proving he wasn't just throwing out terms that he believed would be well received but didn't fully understand. In doing so, Schultz underscored the informed and inclusive corporate culture he helped foster during his decades at the helm.

Missteps

Schultz used language in the CBS interview that some viewers could have interpreted as portraying the store manager as the victim. He told King, "She recognizes that perhaps that call shouldn't have been made." Perhaps? Not exactly the description of someone who is truly remorseful for their actions.

He also said, "I don't think she intended . . . for the police to arrive and arrest the two men," which is a little far-fetched when you consider she acted as if there was a true emergency. Only when pushed does Schultz concede "she regrets calling 911."

DEBRIEF

On May 2, Starbucks announces a financial settlement. The press release is titled "Statement from Starbucks CEO Kevin Johnson, Donte Robinson and Rashon Nelson." Nothing communicates unity more than a joint statement from those previously on opposite sides of a crisis. Typically, the aggrieved won't consent to a joint statement unless they're truly satisfied with the outcome, which Starbucks had worked hard to achieve. Far from transactional, the message sounded like it was just the beginning of a dialogue with the two men. Among the messages:

Starbucks Coffee Company reached a settlement agreement earlier
this week that will allow both sides to move forward and continue
to talk and explore means of preventing similar occurrences at any
Starbucks location.

The agreement . . . includes . . . a commitment to continued
listening and dialogue between the parties as a means toward
developing specific actions and opportunities.

As Johnson said previously, "I want to thank Donte and Rashon
for their willingness to reconcile. I welcome the opportunity to
begin a relationship with them to share learnings and experiences.
And Starbucks will continue to take actions that stem from this
incident to repair and reaffirm our values and vision for the kind of
company we want to be."

In statements announcing a settlement, specific financial details are
typically included in the lead. In this release, the opening used phrases
such as *move forward* and *continue to talk*. The actual resolution isn't
mentioned until the second paragraph. What you prioritize in communications very often reflects the level of importance you assign to those
elements in real life.

In a crisis that easily could have been viewed as a David and Goliath struggle, one of the most successful companies on the planet left no
doubt that it was Starbucks who owed Robinson and Nelson an apology
and not the other way around.

•   •   •

Although some in the media were surprised at how well Starbucks
responded to the crisis, those who had followed the brand for years and
truly understood its reputation capital were not. Consider that Starbucks
lists the following among its values:

- creating a culture of warmth and belonging, where everyone
  is welcome

- being present, connecting with transparency, dignity, and respect

- delivering our very best in all we do, holding ourselves accountable for results[38]

Regardless of the crisis, these values are a pretty good foundation on which to build a response. Sure, some of the brand's attempts at fostering an inclusive and welcoming community have fallen somewhat flat. For example, the Race Together initiative of 2015, which asked employees to engage customers on racial issues by having baristas write the phrase *Race Together* on Starbucks cups, while well intended, was widely criticized as "tone-deaf and patronizing."[39]

While some of Starbucks' past efforts may not have had the desired outcome, the brand deserves credit for trying. After all, few companies have demonstrated a fraction of the employee-first values that Starbucks has over the years. Schultz always made it clear his company was willing to prioritize long-term values over short-term profit. That alone is saying something significant.

Brewing for a Fight

In March 2022, Kevin Johnson announced his retirement from Starbucks, only to be replaced (on an interim basis) by the former CEO Schultz, after five years as chairman. This leadership transition took place at, perhaps, the most crucial juncture in the company's history. As of this writing, 28 US Starbucks stores have voted to unionize, and at least 223 more (of the approximately 9,000 company-operated stores in the US) in 31 states have filed petitions for union elections.[40]

Starbucks' image as an employee-first company is being seriously tested by recent complaints filed by the National Labor Relations Board on behalf of employees who believe they've been mistreated, along with Schultz's reputed history of hard-ball tactics in his attempts to quash unionization efforts. It remains to be seen how Schultz and the brand respond, and if the coffee giant's progressive reputation, nurtured over decades, can weather this latest storm.

EPILOGUE

MUCH LIKE A RESPONSE to protect and defend a reputation, the practice of crisis and issues management itself is never static. It will continue to look and sound different as it reflects shifting societal norms, emerging technologies, and evolving business practices.

Additionally, no one plan and no one response makes sense for every organization. The strategy must be appropriate for the nature of the crisis, the culture of the organization, and the expectations of stakeholders. Some brands will favor a more aggressive approach in ways we have discussed: holding a sit-down interview with a reporter or sending out a statement proactively to media outlets. Other approaches will lean more conservative: sending a brief statement only to those who inquire and using more subdued language.

I do hope, by considering some of the lessons, examples, and advice offered within these pages, you'll be able to successfully navigate whatever reputational crises you and your team confront. Most important: follow your true north, weigh multiple opinions—including those of a seasoned communications professional—and choose the response that won't compound the damage, but will pave the road to redemption.

NOTES

INTRODUCTION

1. *Overpressurization of Natural Gas Distribution System, Explosions, and Fires in Merrimack Valley, Massachusetts*, September 13, 2018, National Transportation Safety Board, adopted September 24, 2019, https://www.ntsb.gov/investigations /AccidentReports/Reports/PAR1902.pdf.

2. Allison DeAngelis, "PR Experts Criticize Columbia Gas' Response to Gas Explosions," *Boston Business Journal*, September 14, 2018, https://www.bizjournals .com/boston/news/2018/09/14/pr-experts-criticize-columbia-gas-response-to -gas.html.

3. US Attorney's Office, District of Massachusetts, "Columbia Gas Sentenced in Connection with September 2018 Gas Explosions in Merrimack Valley," news release, June 23, 2020, https://www.justice.gov/usao-ma/pr/columbia-gas -sentenced-connection-september-2018-gas-explosions-merrimack-valley.

CHAPTER 1

1. Jill Goldsmith, "Disney CEO Bob Chapek to Host Parks-Focused Orlando Investor Event as Wall Street Turns to Business Amid Controversy," *Deadline*, March 25, 2022, https://deadline.com/2022/03/disney-bob-chapek-dont-say-gay-florida -orlando-walt-disney-world-1234986664/.

2. Adam B. Vary, "Disney CEO Bob Chapek Apologizes to LGBTQ Employees, Announces Pause for Political Donations in Florida," *Variety*, March 11, 2022, https://variety.com/2022/film/news/disney-bob-chapek-dont-say-gay-apology -lgbtq-employees-1235202253/.

3. AccountingTools, s.v. "Soft Asset Definition," February 27, 2022, https://www .accountingtools.com/articles/2017/10/30/soft-asset.

4. Weber Shandwick in partnership with KRC Research, *The State of Corporate Reputation in 2020: Everything Matters Now,* January 14, 2020, https://www.webershandwick.com/news/corporate-reputation-2020-everything-matters-now/.

5. Michael Luca, "Reviews, Reputation, and Revenue: The Case of Yelp.com" (Working Paper 12-016, Harvard Business School, Cambridge, MA, 2016), https://www.hbs.edu/ris/Publication%20Files/12-016_a7e4a5a2-03f9-490d-b093-8f951238dba2.pdf.

6. "Comic Cowardice or False Power" (with Lucy Prebble), October 31, 2021, in *Succession,* produced by HBO, podcast, 36:41, https://podcasts.apple.com/us/podcast/comic-cowardice-or-false-power-with-lucy-prebble/id1522790936?i=1000540327059.

7. Cecilia Kang, Matthew Rosenberg, and Mike Isaac, "Mark Zuckerberg Defends Facebook as Furor over Its Tactics Grows," *New York Times,* November 15, 2018, https://www.nytimes.com/2018/11/15/technology/zuckerberg-facebook-sandberg-tactics.html.

8. Alex Woodward, "Zuckerberg Dismisses Facebook's Role in Polarising US, Blaming 'Political and Media Environment,'" *Independent,* March 25, 2021, https://www.independent.co.uk/news/world/americas/us-politics/facebook-mark-zuckerberg-testimony-b1822496.html.

9. John N. Frank, "Viva!USA Push Forces Whole Foods Change," *PR Week,* November 03, 2003, https://www.prweek.com/article/1247320/vivausa-push-forces-whole-foods-change.

10. Maren Keeley and Meghan French Dunbar, CCMedia, "Interview: Whole Foods CEO John Mackey on How He Built a Sustainable Food Empire," SOCAP Digital, January 3, 2015, https://socapglobal.com/2015/01/interview-whole-foods-ceo-john-mackey-on-how-he-built-a-sustainable-food-empire/.

11. Statista, "Net Sales of Whole Foods Market Worldwide from 2010 to 2017," accessed April 23, 2021, https://www.statista.com/statistics/258673/net-sales-of-whole-foods-market-worldwide/.

12. Cision, *Cision's 2019 Global State of the Media Report,* April 23, 2019, https://www.cision.com/resources/white-papers/2019-sotm/.

13. Kate Gardiner, "The Story behind 'The Furrow,' the World's Oldest Content Marketing," *Contently,* October 3, 2013, https://contently.com/2013/10/03/the-story-behind-the-furrow-2/.

14. Marc Benioff, "We Need a New Capitalism," opinion, *New York Times,* October 14, 2019, https://www.nytimes.com/2019/10/14/opinion/benioff-salesforce-capitalism.html.

15. Kara Swisher and Stephanie Ruhle, "Bonus: Marc Benioff at Code Conference 2021," October 4, 2021, *New York Magazine* and Vox Media, Pivot podcast, 48:58, https://podcasts.apple.com/us/podcast/bonus-episode-marc-benioff-at-code-conference-2021/id1073226719?i=1000538046966.

16. Phil Wahba and Julie Steenhuysen, "CVS Becomes First Big U.S. Drugstore Chain to Drop Tobacco," Reuters, February 5, 2014, https://www.reuters.com /article/us-cvscaremark-cigarettes/cvs-becomes-first-big-u-s-drugstore-chain -to-drop-tobacco-idUSBREA140RP20140205.

17. Elizabeth Landau, "CVS Stores to Stop Selling Tobacco," CNN, February 5, 2014, https://www.cnn.com/2014/02/05/health/cvs-cigarettes/index.html.

18. Landau, "CVS Stores."

19. Statista, "Number of Monthly Active Facebook Users Worldwide as of 2nd Quar- ter 2021," accessed January 4, 2021, https://www.statista.com/statistics/264810 /number-of-monthly-active-facebook-users-worldwide/.

20. John Gramlich, "10 Facts about Americans and Facebook," Pew Research Center, June 1, 2021, https://www.pewresearch.org/fact-tank/2021/06/01/facts -about-americans-and-facebook/.

21. Sara Lebow, "Facebook Still Accounts for Nearly a Quarter of US Digital Ad Spending," *Insider Intelligence*, October 20, 2021, https://www.emarketer.com /content/facebook-still-accounts-quarter-of-us-digital-ad-spending.

22. Kali Hays, "Facebook Is Paying a 'Brand Tax' to Hire Tech Workers Who Fear a Black Mark on Their Careers If They Work at the Company," *Business Insider*, January 4, 2022, https://www.businessinsider.com/facebook-pays-brand-tax-hire -talent-fears-career-black-mark-2021-12.

23. Hays, "Facebook Is Paying."

24. Cecilia Kang, "A Facebook Antitrust Suit Can Move Forward, a Judge Says, in a Win for the F.T.C.," *New York Times*, January 11, 2022, https://www.nytimes.com /2022/01/11/technology/facebook-antitrust-ftc.html.

25. Alex Sherman, "Facebook's $232 Billion Fall Sets Record for Largest One-Day Value Drop in Stock Market History," CNBC, February 3, 2022, https://www .cnbc.com/2022/02/03/facebooks-232billion-drop-in-value-sets-all-time-record .html.

CHAPTER 2

1. Associated Press, "Anonymous Sources," accessed October 30, 2020, https:// www.ap.org/about/news-values-and-principles/telling-the-story/anonymous -sources.

2. Jennifer Ryan, "Activision CEO Takes 99.9% Pay Cut until Gender Goals Are Met," *Bloomberg Equality*, October 28, 2021, https://www.bloomberg.com/news /articles/2021-10-28/activision-ceo-requests-lower-pay-until-gender-goals -are-met.

3. Kirsten Grind, Ben Fritz, and Sarah E. Needleman, "Activision CEO Bobby Kotick Knew for Years about Sexual-Misconduct Allegations at Videogame Giant," *Wall Street Journal*, November 16, 2021, https://www.wsj.com /articles/activision-videogames-bobby-kotick-sexual-misconduct-allegations -11637075680.

4. Kirsten Grind, Ben Fritz, and Sarah E. Needleman, "Activision Blizzard CEO Bobby Kotick Tells Colleagues He Would Consider Leaving If He Can't Quickly Fix Problems," *Wall Street Journal*, November 21, 2021, https://www.wsj.com /articles/activision-blizzard-ceo-bobby-kotick-tells-colleagues-he-would -consider-leaving-if-he-cant-quickly-fix-problems-11637533064.

5. Peter Dizikes, "Study: On Twitter, False News Travels Faster Than True Stories," *MIT News*, March 8, 2018, https://news.mit.edu/2018/study-twitter-false-news -travels-faster-true-stories-0308.

6. Jennifer K. Robbennolt, "Apologies and Legal Settlement: An Empirical Examination," *Michigan Law Review* 102, no. 3 (2003): 406, https://repository.law .umich.edu/mlr/vol102/iss3/3.

7. "4 Words Led to Settlement of Woods' Case against Kent," *Johnston Sun Rise*, December 3, 2009, https://johnstonsunrise.net/stories/4-words-led-to -settlement-of-woods-case-against-kent,48506.

8. Diane Curtis, "Sometimes, an Apology Can Deter a Lawsuit," *California Bar Journal*, https://www.calbarjournal.com/July2010/TopHeadlines/TH1.aspx.

9. Jonny Evans, "Apple Statement on iPhone 4 Reception Flaw," *Computerworld*, June 25, 2010, https://www.computerworld.com/article/2468428/apple -statement-on-iphone-4-reception-flaw.html.

10. Avery Hartmans, "Antennagate Just Turned 10. Here's How the iPhone 4's Antenna Issues Became One of Apple's Biggest Scandals of All Time," *Insider*, July 18, 2020, https://www.businessinsider.com/apple-antennagate-scandal -timeline-10-year-anniversary-2020-7.

11. Anita Lienert, "Tesla Autopilot Crash a 'Statistical Inevitability,' Company Says," *Edmunds*, July 7, 2016, https://www.edmunds.com/car-news/tesla-autopilot -crash-a-statistical-inevitability-company-says.html.

12. Eric Newcomer, "In Video, Uber CEO Argues with Driver over Falling Fares," *Bloomberg*, February 28, 2017, https://www.bloomberg.com/news/articles /2017-02-28/in-video-uber-ceo-argues-with-driver-over-falling-fares.

13. Robert Gehrke and Paul Beebe, "Murray's Meltdown: Angry, Rambling Briefing Draws Rebukes," *Salt Lake Tribune*, August 8, 2007, https://archive.sltrib.com /article.php?id=6570325&itype=NGPSID.

14. Robert Gehrke and Paul Beebe, "In Utah Mine Disaster, Bob Murray's Pugnacity a Story in Itself," *Athens News*, September 30, 2007, https://www.athensnews .com/news/local/in-utah-mine-disaster-bob-murrays-pugnacity-a-story-in-itself /article_fd580a64-ae4f-5d44-baf6-c31883a968e4.html.

15. US Food and Drug Administration, "FDA Investigates Multistate Outbreak of E. coli O26 Infections Linked to Chipotle Mexican Grill Restaurants," February 1, 2016, https://www.fda.gov/food/outbreaks-foodborne-illness/fda -investigates-multistate-outbreak-e-coli-o26-infections-linked-chipotle -mexican -grill-restaurants.

16. Sarah Whitten, "Analysts Foresee 24% Dip in Chipotle Stock Price," CNBC, February 23, 2016, https://www.cnbc.com/2016/02/23/analysts-foresee-24-dip -in-chipotle-stock-price.html.

17. Austin Carr, "Chipotle Eats Itself," *Fast Company*, October 16, 2016, https:// www.fastcompany.com/3064068/chipotle-eats-itself.

18. Scott Stump, "Chipotle CEO Speaks Out after Health Scares: This Will Be the Safest Place to Eat," *Today*, December 10, 2015, https://www.today.com/news /chipotle-ceo-speaks-out-after-health-scares-will-be-safest-t60746.

19. Reuters, "Chipotle's Food-Safety Pledge Bumps Stock Price Up 5 Percent," *New York Times*, December 10, 2015, https://www.nytimes.com/2015/12/11/business /chipotles-food-safety-pledge-bumps-stock-price-up-5-percent.html.

20. University of Missouri–Columbia, "Honesty Can Keep Companies' Stock Prices Up during Hard Times," *ScienceDaily*, May 26, 2015 http://www.sciencedaily .com/releases/2015/05/150526132359.htm.

21. Michael Cieply and Brooks Barnes, "Sony Pictures Demands That News Agencies Delete 'Stolen' Data," *New York Times*, December 14, 2014, https://www .nytimes.com/2014/12/15/business/sony-pictures-demands-that-news -organizations-delete-stolen-data.html.

22. Arik Hesseldahl, "Here's Sony Lawyer's Letter Telling Publishers to Stop Publishing Leaks," *Vox Recode*, December 14, 2014, https://www.vox.com/2014/12/14 /11633802/sony-demands-end-to-publishing-leaks-from-stolen-data.

23. University of Denver, Sturm College of Law, "Legal Glossary," by Sheila Hyatt, accessed September 25, 2020, https://www.law.du.edu/index.php/law -school-learning-aids/legal-language.

24. Jaikumar Vijayan, "TJX Data Breach: At 45.6M Card Numbers, It's the Biggest Ever," *ComputerWorld*, March 29, 2007, https://www.computerworld.com /article/2544306/tjx-data-breach--at-45-6m-card-numbers--it-s-the-biggest -ever.html.

25. Bob Bragdon, "TJX: How Not to Handle a Crisis," *CSO Online*, March 1, 2007, https://www.csoonline.com/article/2121200/tjx--how-not-to-handle-a-crisis.html.

26. Terry Nguyen, "Why Are Brands So Bad at Apologizing?," *Vox*, November 14, 2019, https://www.vox.com/the-goods/2019/11/14/20961662/brand -apology-sorry.

27. Steve Heisler, "Is a Company Apology Always Necessary?," *American Marketing Association*, April 9, 2020, https://www.ama.org/marketing-news/is-a -company-apology-always-necessary/.

28. Dove, "An image we recently posted," Twitter post, October 7, 2017, 11:27 a.m., https://twitter.com/dove/status/916731793927278592?lang=en.

29. Stuart Mitchell, "Past Campaigns—The Dove Self-Esteem Project," *Ethical Marketing News*, March 26, 2017, https://ethicalmarketingnews.com/past -campaigns-dove-self-esteem-project.

30. "Model in 'Racist' Dove Ad Speaks Out," BBC, October 11, 2017, https://www
.bbc.com/news/newsbeat-41586402.

31. Mike Snider and Charisse Jones, "Dove Ad Underscores Tense Cultural
Moment for Advertisers," *USA Today*, October 9, 2017, https://www
.usatoday.com/story/money/business/2017/10/09/dove-ad-underscores
-tense-cultural-moment-advertisers/745543001/.

CHAPTER 3

1. Seth Arenstein, "62% Have Crisis Plans, but Few Update Them or Practice
Scenarios," *PR News*, February 5, 2020, https://www.prnewsonline.com/crisis
-survey-CSA-practice.

2. Tara Siegel Bernard et al., "Equifax Says Cyberattack May Have Affected 143
Million in the U.S.," *New York Times*, September 7, 2017, https://www.nytimes
.com/2017/09/07/business/equifax-cyberattack.html.

3. Bernard et al., "Equifax Cyberattack."

4. Aimee Picchi, "Equifax Breach Response Criticized for Waits, Lawsuit Waiver,"
CBS News, September 8, 2017, https://www.cbsnews.com/news/equifax-breach
-response-criticized-for-wait-lawsuit-waiver/.

5. Kevin Dugan, "Equifax Blames Giant Breach on Vendor Software Flaw," *New
York Post*, September 8, 2017, https://nypost.com/2017/09/08/equifax-blames
-giant-breach-on-vendor-software-flaw/.

6. Maggie Fitzgerald, "Robinhood CEO Says It Limited Buying in GameStop to
'Protect the Firm and Protect Our Customers," CNBC, January 28, 2021, https://
www.cnbc.com/2021/01/28/robinhood-ceo-says-it-limited-buying-in-gamestop
-to-protect-the-firm-and-protect-our-customers.html.

7. Lance Lambert, "Robinhood's Brand Is Severely Damaged: 56% of Account
Holders Are Considering Leaving the App," *Fortune*, February 19, 2021, https://
fortune.com/2021/02/19/robinhood-brand-damage-gamestop-hedge-funds
-wallstreetbets-reddit-stocks-gme-amc/.

8. K. Michael Cummings, Anthony Brown, and Richard O'Connor, "The Cigarette
Controversy," *Cancer Epidemiology, Biomarkers, and Prevention* 16, no. 6 (June
2007): 1070–76, https://cebp.aacrjournals.org/content/16/6/1070.

9. US Food and Drug Administration, "FDA Proposes New Health Warnings
for Cigarette Packs and Ads," accessed August 24, 2021, https://www.fda
.gov/tobacco-products/labeling-and-warning-statements-tobacco-products
/fda-proposes-new-health-warnings-cigarette-packs-and-ads.

10. Karu F. Daniels, "Amid COVID-19 Pandemic, Giant Food Supermarket Chain
Apologizes for Tone-Deaf 'Super Spread' Circular Ad," *New York Daily News*,
November 18, 2020, https://www.nydailynews.com/news/national/ny
-coronavirus-giant-food-supermarket-apologize-super-spread-ad-20201118
-33sja5v7cfha5dfuzyh5zfyilq-story.html.

CHAPTER 4

1. Rick Porter, "TV Long View: A Guide to the Ever-Expanding World of Ratings Data," *Hollywood Reporter*, October 5, 2019, https://www.hollywoodreporter .com/tv/tv-news/tv-ratings-explained-a-guide-what-data-all-means-1245591/.

2. Mike Cannon-Brookes, "The Standard You Walk Past Is the Standard You Accept," *Atlassian*, June 1, 2020, https://www.atlassian.com/blog /announcements/the-standard-you-walk-past-is-the-standard-you-accept.

3. Katie Weston, "Furniture Village Is Hit by a Week-Long Cyber-Attack Leaving Customers 'with Nothing to Sit On' and Unable to Pay as They Wait for Sofas, Beds and Tables," *Daily Mail*, June 4, 2021, https://www.dailymail.co.uk/news /article-9651569/Furniture-Village-hit-cyber-attack-leaving-customers-sit -unable-pay.html.

4. Gini Dietrich, "What Is the PESO Model?" CommPRO, accessed September 1, 2020, https://www.commpro.biz/what-is-the-peso-model/.

5. James R. Healey, "Study: 303 Deaths in GM Cars with Airbag Failure," *USA Today*, March 23, 2014, https://www.usatoday.com/story/money/cars/2014/03/13 /gm-recall-death-nhtsa-airbag/6401257/.

6. Fred Meier, "Video: GM CEO Barra Says, 'Something Went Wrong,'" *USA Today*, March 17, 2014, https://www.usatoday.com/story/money/cars/2014/03/17/gm -ceo-mary-barra-recalls/6529007/.

7. Meier, "Video: GM CEO Barra."

8. NHS England, "NHS Support via Text Message for People with Symptoms of Covid-19," March 28, 2020, https://www.england.nhs.uk/2020/03/nhs -support-via-text-message-people-with-symptoms-of-covid-19/.

9. Gartner, Digital Channel Survey 2016, July 14, 2016, accessible at https://www .gartner.com/en/documents/3379017.

CHAPTER 5

1. Seth Arenstein, "62% Have Crisis Plans, but Few Update Them or Practice Scenarios," *PR News*, February 5, 2020, https://www.prnewsonline.com/crisis -survey-CSA-practice.

2. See, for example, Small Business Administration, "Prepare for Emergencies," accessed December 27, 2021, https://www.sba.gov/business-guide/manage -your-business/prepare-emergencies.

CHAPTER 6

1. John Halusha, "Exxon's Public Relations Problem," *New York Times*, April 21, 1989, https://www.nytimes.com/1989/04/21/business/exxon-s-public-relations -problem.html.

2. Herminia Ibarra, "The Authenticity Paradox," *Harvard Business Review*, January–February 2015, https://hbr.org/2015/01/the-authenticity-paradox.

3. A. J. Willingham, "How 'Thoughts and Prayers' Went from Common Condolence to Cynical Meme," CNN, May 19, 2018, https://www.cnn.com/2018/02/20 /us/thoughts-and-prayers-florida-school-shooting-trnd/index.html.

4. Diana Kawarsky, *Soft Skills Volume 1: A Collection of Strategies, Anecdotes, Techniques, Observations, Stories, Tactics, Advice, Experiences, Ideas, and Methods*, Lulu Publishing Services, April 5, 2016.

CHAPTER 7

1. Gus Lubin, "BP CEO Tony Hayward Apologizes for His Idiotic Statement: 'I'd Like My Life Back,'" *Business Insider*, June 2, 2010, https://www.businessinsider .com/bp-ceo-tony-hayward-apologizes-for-saying-id-like-my-life-back-2010-6.

2. Julia Carrie Wong, "Facebook Finally Responds to New Zealand on Christchurch Attack," *Guardian*, March 29, 2019, https://www.theguardian.com /us-news/2019/mar/29/facebook-new-zealand-christchurch-attack-response.

3. Colonial Pipeline, "Media Statement Update: Colonial Pipeline System Disruption," press release, May 17, 2021, 5:25 p.m., https://www.colpipe.com/news /press-releases/media-statement-colonial-pipeline-system-disruption.

4. Christopher Bing and Stephanie Kelly, "Cyber-attack Shuts Down U.S. Fuel Pipeline 'Jugular,' Biden Briefed," Reuters, May 28, 2021, https://www.reuters.com /technology/colonial-pipeline-halts-all-pipeline-operations-after-cybersecurity -attack-2021-05-08/.

5. Alyssa G. Millner, Shari R. Veil, and Timothy L. Sellnow, "Proxy Communication in Crisis Response," *Public Relations Review* 37, no. 1 (March 2011): 74–76, https://doi.org/10.1016/j.pubrev.2010.10.005.

6. US Federal Drug Administration, "Guidance for Industry: Measures to Address the Risk for Contamination by Salmonella Species in Food Containing a Peanut-Derived Product as an Ingredient," March 2009, https://www.fda.gov /regulatory-information/search-fda-guidance-documents/guidance-industry -measures-address-risk-contamination-salmonella-species-food-containing -peanut.

7. Brady Dennis, "Executive Who Shipped Tainted Peanuts Gets 28 Years; 9 Died of Salmonella," *Washington Post*, September 21, 2015, https://www.washingtonpost .com/national/health-science/a-life-sentence-for-shipping-tainted-peanuts -victims-families-say-yes/2015/09/19/e844a314-5bf1-11e5-8e9e-dce8a2a2a679 _story.html.

8. Rheana Murray, "Lululemon CEO Apologizes after Saying Not All Women Should Wear the Brand's Yoga Pants," *New York Daily News*, November 13, 2013, https://www.nydailynews.com/life-style/fashion/lululemon-ceo-pants-gaffe -article-1.1515476.

9. Jon Harmon, "A Disaster at Dealing with Catastrophe," *Los Angeles Times*, August 21, 2007, https://www.latimes.com/archives/la-xpm-2007-aug-21-oe -harmon21-story.html.

10. Mentalhelp.net, "Stress Inoculation Therapy," accessed December 22, 2020, https://www.mentalhelp.net/stress/inoculation-therapy/.

CHAPTER 8

1. Steven Pearlstein, "'No Comment': The Death of Business Reporting," *Washington Post*, July 6, 2018, https://www.washingtonpost.com/business/no-comment-the-death-of-business-reporting/2018/07/06/4fbca852-7e31-11e8-bb6b-c1cb691f1402_story.html.

2. Carmine Gallo, "How Presidential Candidates Prepare to Look Spontaneous," *Forbes*, August 6, 2015, https://www.forbes.com/sites/carminegallo/2015/08/06/how-presidential-candidates-prepare-to-look-spontaneous/?sh=6158a766fb15.

CHAPTER 9

1. Tara Siegel Barnard, "In Retreat, Bank of America Cancels Debit Card Fee," *New York Times*, November 1, 2011, https://www.nytimes.com/2011/11/02/business/bank-of-america-drops-plan-for-debit-card-fee.html.

2. Sapna Maheshwari, "She Was a Candidate to Lead Levi's. Then She Started Tweeting," *New York Times*, March 25, 2022, https://www.nytimes.com/2022/03/25/business/levis-jen-sey.html.

3. Brian Braiker, "American Apparel Apologizes for Use of Challenger Explosion Photo," *Digiday*, July 4, 2014, https://digiday.com/marketing/american-apparel-apologize-offensive-use-challenger-explosion-photo/.

4. Jennifer Calfas, "Adidas Apologizes after Sending 'You Survived' Email to Boston Marathon Finishers," *Time*, April 18, 2017, https://time.com/4745066/adidas-boston-marathon-email/.

5. "Kenneth Cole Apologizes for Tweet Using Egypt Protests to Promote Fashion Line," *Los Angeles Times*, February 4, 2011, https://latimesblogs.latimes.com/technology/2011/02/kenneth-cole-tweet-on-egypt-protests-sparks-controversy-.html.

6. Sprout Social, "The Sprout Social Index, Edition XII: Call-Out Culture, 2017," accessed November 25, 2021, https://sproutsocial.com/insights/data/q3-2017/.

7. Conor Shine, "What Businesses Can Learn from Southwest's Social Media Response during Its Tech Outage," *Dallas Morning News*, August 5, 2016, https://www.dallasnews.com/business/local-companies/2016/08/05/what-businesses-can-learn-from-southwest-s-social-media-response-during-its-tech-outage/.

8. Shine, "What Businesses Can Learn."

9. Shine, "What Businesses Can Learn."

10. Southwest Airlines, Twitter feed, July 20, 2016, https://twitter.com/southwestair/status/755860294874730496.

11. Southwest Airines, Twitter post, reply to Jill Marie, July 20, 2016, https://twitter.com/southwestair/status/755838425274515456.

12. Southwest Airines, Twitter post, reply to Doc Rissa, July 20, 2016, https://twitter .com/docrissado/status/755860916734873601?ref_src=twsrc%5Etfw.

13. Mary Beth Quirk, "Southwest CEO Compares Major Outage to 'Once-in-a-Thousand-Year' Flood," *Consumerist*, August 1, 2016, https://consumerist.com /2016/08/01/southwest-ceo-compares-major-outage-to-once-in-a-thousand-year -flood/.

14. Southwest Airlines, Twitter post, July 21, 2016, 4:55 a.m., https://twitter.com /southwestair/status/756095345428344832.

15. Southwest Airlines, Twitter feed, July 20, 2016, https://twitter.com/southwestair /status/755860294874730496.

16. Southwest Airlines Twitter Feed, July 20, 2016.

17. Southwest Airlines Twitter Feed, July 20, 2016.

CHAPTER 10

1. Adam Harris, "Cosby's Honorary Degree Is the First Yale Has Rescinded in 300 -Plus Years," *The Atlantic*, May 2, 2018, https://www.theatlantic.com/education /archive/2018/05/yale-bill-cosby-honorary-degree/559490/.

2. Ruth Bruno, "Wesleyan University Revokes Bill Cosby's Honorary Degree," *Hartford Courant*, May 25, 2018, https://www.courant.com/breaking-news /hc-br-wesleyan-revokes-honorary-degree-20180525-story.html.

3. Josh Logue, "Rush to Revoke (or Not)," *Inside Higher Ed*, October 28, 2015, https://www.insidehighered.com/news/2015/10/28/colleges-continue-rescind -cosbys-honorary-degrees.

4. Sydney Ember and Colin Moynihan, "To Revoke or Not: Colleges That Gave Cosby Honors Face a Tough Question," *New York Times*, October 6, 2015, https://www.nytimes.com/2015/10/07/arts/television/to-revoke-or-not-colleges -that-gave-cosby-honors-face-a-tough-question.html.

5. Elizabeth A. Harris, "The Met Will Turn Down Sackler Money amid Fury over the Opioid Crisis," *New York Times*, May 15, 2019, https://www.nytimes.com /2019/05/15/arts/design/met-museum-sackler-opioids.html.

6. Peggy McGlone, "Citing Opioid Ties, the Met Says It Will No Longer Accept Gifts from the Sackler Family," *Washington Post*, May 15, 2019, https://www .washingtonpost.com/entertainment/museums/citing-opioid-ties-the-met-says -it-will-no-longer-accept-gifts-from-the-sackler-family/2019/05/15/e66ac2d8 -7742-11e9-b7ae-390de4259661_story.html.

7. Steve Dubb, "The Met Says It Won't Accept More Sackler Money, but Sackler Name Remains," *Non-Profit Quarterly*, May 17, 2019, https://nonprofitquarterly .org/the-met-says-it-wont-accept-more-sackler-money-but-sackler-name -remains/.

8. Sarah Cascone, "After Purdue Pharma Reached a $225 Million Settlement with US Authorities, the Met Says the Name of Its Sackler Wing Is 'Under Review,'" *Artnet News*, October 23, 2020, https://news.artnet.com/art-world/sacklers-name -museum-met-1917814.

9. Sharon Otterman and Hannah Dreyfus, "Michael Steinhardt, a Leader in Jewish Philanthropy, Is Accused of a Pattern of Sexual Harassment," *New York Times*, March 21, 2019, https://www.nytimes.com/2019/03/21/nyregion/michael -steinhardt-sexual-harassment.html.

10. Victor Porcelli, "Steinhardt Name to Stay Despite Allegations of Sexual Harassment," *Washington Square News*, September 12, 2019, https://nyunews.com/news /2019/09/12/michael-steinhardt-name-change-school-nyu/.

CHAPTER 11

1. Tori DeAngelis, "In Search of Cultural Competence," *Monitor on Psychology* 46, no. 3 (March 2015): 64, https://www.apa.org/monitor/2015/03/cultural -competence.

2. Amanda Mull, "Brands Have Nothing Real to Say about Racism," *The Atlantic*, June 3, 2020, https://www.theatlantic.com/health/archive/2020/06/brands -racism-protests-amazon-nfl-nike/612613/.

3. David Von Drehle, "Opinion: Corporations' Quick Shunning of Russia Showcases the New Morality of Doing Business," *Washington Post*, March 11, 2022, https://www.washingtonpost.com/opinions/2022/03/11/corporate-withdrawal -from-russia-signals-new-morality/.

4. Steve Dent, "Apple and Foxconn Admit to Hiring Too Many Temporary Workers," *Engadget*, September 9, 2019, https://www.engadget.com/2019-09-09-apple -foxconn-temporary-workers-china.html.

5. GLAAD, *GLAAD Media Reference Guide: Terms to Avoid*, accessed October 25, 2020, https://www.glaad.org/reference/terms.

6. Laura Krantz and Deirdre Fernandes, "BU President Apologizes for Initial Letter on Racism, Sends a Second," *Boston Globe*, updated June 3, 2020, https://www .bostonglobe.com/2020/06/03/metro/bu-president-apologizes-initial-letter -racism-sends-second/?event=event12.

7. Krantz and Fernandes, "BU President Apologizes."

8. Sally Ho, "'Empty Words': Companies Touting Black Lives Matter Accused of Hypocrisy," Associated Press, June 11, 2020, https://komonews.com/news/local /empty-words-companies-touting-black-lives-matter-accused-of.

9. Ho, "'Empty Words.'"

10. Ho, "'Empty Words.'"

11. Ho, "'Empty Words.'"

12. Ho, "'Empty Words.'"

13. Jon Chesto, "With Nationwide Fellowship Program, PwC's US Chief Ramps Up Racial Equity Effort," *Boston Globe*, October 5, 2020, https://www.bostonglobe .com/2020/10/05/business/with-nationwide-fellowship-program-pwcs-us-chief -ramps-up-racial-equity-effort/.

14. CEO Action for Diversity and Inclusion, home page, accessed February 10, 2022, https://www.ceoaction.com/.

15. Adam Farley, "Tim Ryan: A Champion for Diversity in the Workplace," *Irish America*, October–November 2017, https://www.irishamerica.com/2017/10 /tim-ryan-a-champion-for-diversity-in-the-workplace/.

CHAPTER 12

1. PwC Global, *Global Crisis Survey 2021*, accessed March 25, 2022, https://www .pwc.com/gx/en/issues/crisis-solutions/global-crisis-survey.html.

CASE STUDIES

1. *PRWeek* Staff, "United Airlines CEO Oscar Munoz Named *PR Week* U.S. Communicator of the Year," *PR Week US*, March 9, 2017, https://www.prweek .com/article/1426909/united-airlines-ceo-oscar-munoz-named-prweek-us -communicator-year.

2. *PRWeek* Staff, "CEO Oscar Munoz."

3. Sean Czarnecki, "Timeline of a Crisis: United Airlines," *PR Week*, June 6, 2017, https://www.prweek.com/article/1435619/timeline-crisis-united-airlines.

4. Daniel Victor and Matt Stevens, "United Airlines Passenger Is Dragged from an Overbooked Flight," *New York Times*, April 10, 2017, https://www.nytimes.com /2017/04/10/business/united-flight-passenger-dragged.html.

5. Irina Ivanova, "United Airlines Passenger Suffered Broken Nose, Concussion," *CBS News*, April 13, 2017, https://www.cbsnews.com/news/united-airlines -passenger-dragged-off-flight-speaks/.

6. Abby Ohlheiser, "The Full Timeline of How Social Media Turned United into the Biggest Story in the Country," *Washington Post*, April 11, 2017, https://www .washingtonpost.com/news/the-intersect/wp/2017/04/11/the-full-timeline-of -how-social-media-turned-united-into-the-biggest-story-in-the-country/.

7. Lucas Aulbach, "Video Shows Man Forcibly Removed from United Flight from Chicago to Louisville," *Courier-Journal*, April 10, 2017, https://www.courier -journal.com/story/news/2017/04/10/video-shows-man-forcibly-removed -united-flight-chicago-louisville/100274374/.

8. AP News, "United CEO's 3 Statements on Passenger Dragged Off Flight," April 11, 2017, https://apnews.com/article/us-news-ap-top-news-chicago-il-state-wire -airlines-01bf37fd33f04cc7a097c9cce5d557fe.

9. Merriam-Webster, s.v. "accommodate (*verb*)," accessed March 25, 2022, https:// www.merriam-webster.com/dictionary/accommodate.

10. Bess Levin, "United C.E.O. Offers the Worst Possible Response to the Airline's P.R. Disaster," *Vanity Fair*, April 11, 2017, https://www.vanityfair.com/news /2017/04/united-airlines-oscar-munoz.

11. AP News, "United CEO's 3 Statements."

12. AP News, "United CEO's 3 Statements."

13. Czarnecki, "Timeline of a Crisis."

14. AP News, "United CEO's 3 Statements."

15. Michael Edison Hayden and Erin Dooley, "United CEO Feels 'Shame,' Passengers Will Be Compensated," ABC News, April 12, 2017, https://abcnews.go.com/US/united-ceo-oscar-munoz-felt-sham-passenger-dragged/story?id=46746594.

16. Hayden and Dooley, "United CEO Feels 'Shame.'"

17. Hayden and Dooley, "United CEO Feels 'Shame.'"

18. Hayden and Dooley, "United CEO Feels 'Shame.'"

19. Melissa Chan, "David Dao's Daughter Says the United Airlines Incident 'Sickened' His Family," Time, April 13, 2017, https://time.com/4738429/david-dao-united-airlines/.

20. Cision, PR Newswire, "United Airlines Announces Changes to Improve Customer Experience," United Airlines press release, April 27, 2017, https://hub.united.com/united-changes-improve-customer-experience-2567373435.html.

21. Danielle Muolo, "The Lawyer for the United Passenger Dragged Off a Plane Is Suddenly Singing the Airline's Praises after Settlement," Insider, April 27, 2017, https://www.businessinsider.com/david-daos-lawyer-praises-united-ceo-for-taking-full-responsibility-2017-4.

22. "United CEO to Congress: 'We Failed' Our Customers and Company," ABC News, May 2, 2017, video, 5:41, https://abcnews.go.com/Politics/video/united-ceo-congress-failed-customers-company-47155872.

23. Lori Aratani, "A Year after the Infamous United Dragging Incident, Has Anything Changed for Airline Travelers?," Washington Post, April 9, 2018, https://www.washingtonpost.com/news/dr-gridlock/wp/2018/04/09/a-year-after-the-infamous-united-dragging-incident-has-anything-changed-for-airlines-travelers/.

24. Jeffrey Cook and Benjamin Siu, "Dog Dies on United Flight after Being Placed in Overhead Bin, Airline Confirms," ABC News, March 13, 2018, https://abcnews.go.com/US/dog-dies-united-flight-overhead-bin-airline-confirms/story?id=53718599.

25. Cook and Siu, "Dog Dies on United Flight."

26. Starbucks, "History of Partner Benefits at Starbucks," July 18, 2016, https://stories.starbucks.com/press/2016/starbucks-history-of-partner-benefits/.

27. Starbucks, "History of Partner Benefits."

28. Kate Taylor, "Starbucks' New CEO Says Social Engagement Is Part of the Company's 'Strategy'—Even When It Gets Controversial," Business Insider Australia, April 3, 2017, https://www.businessinsider.com.au/starbucks-social-initiatives-are-strategic-2017-3.

29. Dominick Proto, "Starbucks Manager Told 911 of 2 Men 'Refusing to Make a Purchase or Leave' before Their Arrests," ABC News, April 18, 2018, https://abcnews.go.com/US/starbucks-manager-told-911-men-refusing-make-purchase/story?id=54555672.

30. Patricia Madej, Joseph N. DiStefano, and Jacob Adelman, "Black Men's Arrests at Philadelphia Starbucks Prompt City Probes amid National Outcry," *Philadelphia Inquirer,* April 14, 2018, https://www.inquirer.com/philly/news/starbucks -philadelphia-police-viral-video-investigation-race-20180414.html.

31. Starbucks, Twitter post, April 14, 2018, 9:59 a.m., https://twitter.com/starbucks /status/985200942030012416?lang=en.

32. Starbucks, "Starbucks CEO: Reprehensible Outcome in Philadelphia Incident," April 14, 2018, https://stories.starbucks.com/press/2018/starbucks-ceo -reprehensible-outcome-in-philadelphia-incident/.

33. Stephanie Farr and Andrew Seidman, "Starbucks CEO in Philadelphia as Pro- tests Resume at Center City Starbucks Where Two Black Men Were Arrested," *Philadelphia Inquirer,* April 15, 2018, https://www.inquirer.com/philly/news /starbucks-philadelphia-police-viral-video-investigation-race-ceo-protest -20180415.html.

34. Farr and Seidman, "Starbucks CEO in Philadelphia."

35. "Starbucks CEO Speaks Out after Black Men Arrested," *Good Morning America,* April 16, 2018, video, 7:14, https://www.goodmorningamerica.com/news/video /starbucks-ceo-speaks-black-men-arrested-54495894.

36. Bill Hutchinson, "Starbucks to Close 8,000 Stores to Give Staff 'Racial Bias' Training," ABC News, April 17, 2018, https://abcnews.go.com/US/starbucks -shop-black-men-arrested-draws-scrutiny-officials/story?id=54526172.

37. Starbucks, "A Preview of the May 29 Curriculum for 175,000 Starbucks Partners across the Country," May 23, 2018, https://stories.starbucks.com/stories/2018 /starbucks-curriculum-preview-for-may-29/.

38. Starbucks, "Culture and Values," accessed December 2, 2020, https://www .starbucks.com/careers/working-at-starbucks/culture-and-values.

39. Kate Taylor, "Howard Schultz Reveals How He Decided to Launch Starbucks' 'Embarrassing' and 'Tone Deaf' Race Together Campaign despite Internal Concerns," *Insider,* January 29, 2019, https://www.businessinsider.com /howard-schultz-failed-race-together-campaign-2019-1.

40. Michael Hiltzik, "Why Starbucks Has Become a Huge Unionization Target— and Why the Company Is in a Panic," *Los Angeles Times,* April 24, 2022, https:// www.latimes.com/business/story/2022-04-24/column-starbucks-union-howard -schulz-long-beach.

ACKNOWLEDGMENTS

1. Kurt Vonnegut Jr., *Wampeters, Foma, and Granfalloons* (New York: Delacorte Press, 1974), xxii.

ACKNOWLEDGMENTS

WRITING, FOR ME, has always held a meditative quality. Why I find it so satisfying can be best described by what the late author and satirist Kurt Vonnegut Jr. claimed he found most encouraging about writing: that it allows "people who are patient and industrious to revise their stupidity, to edit themselves into something like intelligence."[1] I do hope you found the concepts and lessons I've shared somewhat intelligent and helpful.

I owe a debt of gratitude to Dan Cence, CEO of Issues Management Group, for his enthusiastic support of this project along with his guidance and encouragement every day. My heartfelt appreciation extends to Helene Solomon and Ashley McCown, whose mentorship in the practice and business of public relations was invaluable. After a career in which I did an awful lot of speaking, Dan, Helene, and Ashley taught me the importance of being a keen listener and calibrating my response and counsel based on what we hear from our clients in their time of need.

Thank you to my literary agent Ken Lizotte for believing I offer a unique perspective that would be of interest to readers. I cannot say enough great things about the collaborative team at Berrett-Koehler, especially editorial director and North Shore expat Neal Maillet, who was a tremendous advocate for this book and helped me zero in on the concept of reputation capital.

I must thank my wife, Kerri, herself an accomplished writer, producer, and editor. Her meticulous review of every word in the manuscript and her candid feedback throughout made this book infinitely more readable and better in every way. Her support and patience throughout this process was invaluable and more than I had a right to ask for.

Keeping it in the family, my brother Eric provided some excellent notes down the homestretch. My gratitude to him, my parents, Richard and Marilyn, and my sister Lindsey for their encouragement in this pursuit.

Finally, thank you to all of my colleagues in television and PR, past and present, who've made every day in the newsroom, at the office, or in the field such an interesting and unpredictable adventure.

INDEX

Note: *italicized* page numbers in index indicate illustrative material.

mock interviews, 109–110
role-playing, 110–111
transitional phrases, 109
transparency, 36–37, 51–52, 94,
97–98, 139, 183
trolling on social media, 131
trustworthiness, and quality
communication, 95–96
truthfulness, importance of, 49
Tumblr, 126
Twitter, 24, 62, 126, 127, 129, 131, 164,
176
Tylenol, 93

U
Uber, 29–30
United Airlines, 35
case study, 163–175
universities, honorary degrees,
135–136
US Food and Drug Administration,
105

V
value
highest values, choosing, 16–17
values
and social issues, 143–144
victim, playing the, 31–33, 106–107
victim naming, 172
victim shaming, 165, 168
video appearances and
communication, 62–63, 64,
180–181
virtue signaling, 15, 142–143
volunteer opportunities, 149
Von Drehle, David, 143
vulnerabilities, potential, of
organizations, 25–26

W
Walgreens, 17
Walsh, Rebecca, 30
Walt Disney Company, 7–8, 9, 105
Warby Parker, 14
websites
apologies on, 178–179
and crisis communication, 59–60
Weiss, Daniel, 138
Wesleyan University, 137
Whole Foods, 12–13, 30, 130
Wilson, Chip, 106–107
Wilson, Rita, 153
Woods, James, 26–27
Woods, Michael, 26–27
working from home, 155
World Central Kitchen, 16
World Health Organization
(WHO), 154
written tools for communication
audience considerations, 77–78
community letters, 83–84
if-then scenarios, 83
media statements, 84–86
strategy, 78–79
timeline, 79–80
wrongdoing and guilt, 27–28

Y
Yelp, 9, 12

Z
Zuckerberg, Mark, 10

ABOUT THE AUTHOR

T.J. Winick leads the Crisis practice at Issues Management Group, an award-winning strategic communications, public affairs, and digital firm based in Boston.

He is regularly relied upon for his counsel on many delicate and high-profile issues, including those involving litigation support, industrial accidents, DEI, executive misconduct, Title IX, and leadership transitions as well as a myriad of crises that have their origin on social media.

This work is performed on behalf of publicly traded companies, small businesses, prestigious nonprofits, independent schools, colleges, and universities. T.J.'s insights on crisis communications have appeared in numerous outlets, including *Forbes*, *PR Week*, *PR News*, and *O'Dwyer's*.

During his two decades as a broadcast journalist, T.J. worked as a news reporter for television network affiliates in Florida, Pittsburgh, and Boston. As a correspondent and anchor for ABC News, he reported across platforms, including *NewsOne*, *Nightline*, *World News*, *Good Morning America*, and *World News Now*.

T.J. graduated with honors from Colby College in Maine. He and his family live north of Boston.

Berrett–Koehler
BK Publishers

Berrett-Koehler is an independent publisher dedicated to an ambitious mission: *Connecting people and ideas to create a world that works for all.*

Our publications span many formats, including print, digital, audio, and video. We also offer online resources, training, and gatherings. And we will continue expanding our products and services to advance our mission.

We believe that the solutions to the world's problems will come from all of us, working at all levels: in our society, in our organizations, and in our own lives. Our publications and resources offer pathways to creating a more just, equitable, and sustainable society. They help people make their organizations more humane, democratic, diverse, and effective (and we don't think there's any contradiction there). And they guide people in creating positive change in their own lives and aligning their personal practices with their aspirations for a better world.

And we strive to practice what we preach through what we call "The BK Way." At the core of this approach is *stewardship,* a deep sense of responsibility to administer the company for the benefit of all of our stakeholder groups, including authors, customers, employees, investors, service providers, sales partners, and the communities and environment around us. Everything we do is built around stewardship and our other core values of *quality, partnership, inclusion,* and *sustainability.*

This is why Berrett-Koehler is the first book publishing company to be both a B Corporation (a rigorous certification) and a benefit corporation (a for-profit legal status), which together require us to adhere to the highest standards for corporate, social, and environmental performance. And it is why we have instituted many pioneering practices (which you can learn about at www.bkconnection.com), including the Berrett-Koehler Constitution, the Bill of Rights and Responsibilities for BK Authors, and our unique Author Days.

We are grateful to our readers, authors, and other friends who are supporting our mission. We ask you to share with us examples of how BK publications and resources are making a difference in your lives, organizations, and communities at www.bkconnection.com/impact.

Dear reader,

Thank you for picking up this book and welcome to the worldwide BK community! You're joining a special group of people who have come together to create positive change in their lives, organizations, and communities.

What's BK all about?

Our mission is to connect people and ideas to create a world that works for all.

Why? Our communities, organizations, and lives get bogged down by old paradigms of self-interest, exclusion, hierarchy, and privilege. But we believe that can change. That's why we seek the leading experts on these challenges—and share their actionable ideas with you.

A welcome gift

To help you get started, we'd like to offer you a **free copy** of one of our bestselling ebooks:

www.bkconnection.com/welcome

When you claim your **free ebook**, you'll also be subscribed to our blog.

Our freshest insights

Access the best new tools and ideas for leaders at all levels on our blog at ideas.bkconnection.com.

Sincerely,

Your friends at Berrett-Koehler

Certified

Corporation